VISITORS' ATLAS &
A-Z DEVON
CORNWALL
WEST SOMERSET

CONTENTS

Geographers' A-Z Map Company Ltd

Fairfield Road, Borough Green,
Sevenoaks, Kent TN15 8PP
Enquiries & Trade Sales
01732 781000
Retail Sales
01732 783422

Edition 4 2005. © Copyright of Geographers' A-Z Map Company Ltd. 2004

2

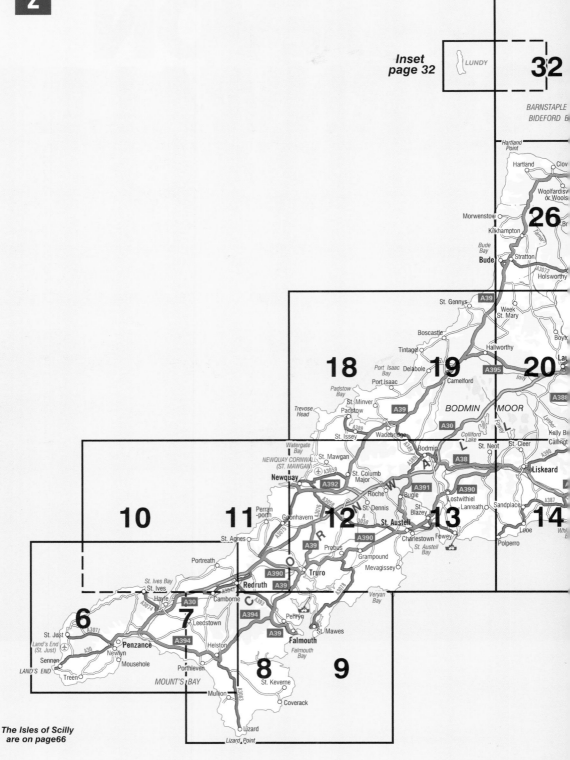

Inset
page 32

LUNDY

32

BARNSTAPLE
BIDEFORD B

Hartland
Point

Hartland   Clov

Woolfardisw
or Wools

Morwenstow

Kilkhampton   **26**   Br

Bude
Bay

St. Gennys

Week
St. Mary

Boscastle

Tintagel   Hallworthy

Port Isaac
Bay   Delabole   **19**   Boyt

Port Isaac

Camelford   **20**   Lau

Padstow
Bay   St. Minver

18   Padstow   A39

Trevose
Head   St. Issey   BODMIN   MOOR   A38

Wadebridge   Colliford
Lake   Kelly Br

St. Neot   St. Cleer   Callingt

Watergate
Bay   Bodmin   A30   A38

NEWQUAY CORNWALL
(ST. MAWGAN)   St. Mawgan   St. Columb
Major   A391   Liskeard

Newquay   A392   Roche   Bugle   Lostwithiel   A390

St. Dennis   St.
Blazey   Lanreath   Sandplace   A387

10   Perran
-porth   **12**   A
3058   St. Austell   **13**   **14**

Goonhavern   A390   Charlestown   Fowey   Looe   Whi
E

St. Agnes   A39   Probus   St. Austell
Bay   Polperro

Portreath   A390   Grampound

St. Ives Bay   Truro   Mevagissey

11   St. Ives   Redruth   A39   Veryan
Bay

Hayle   Camborne

6   A30   Leedstown   A394

Penryn

7   Penryn   St. Mawes

St. Just   Penzance   A394   Helston   Falmouth

Land's End
(St. Just)   Newlyn   Falmouth
Bay

Sennen

LAND'S END   Mousehole   Porthleven   **8**   **9**

Treen   St. Keverne

MOUNT'S BAY   Mullion

Coverack

Lizard

The Isles of Scilly
are on page66   Lizard Point

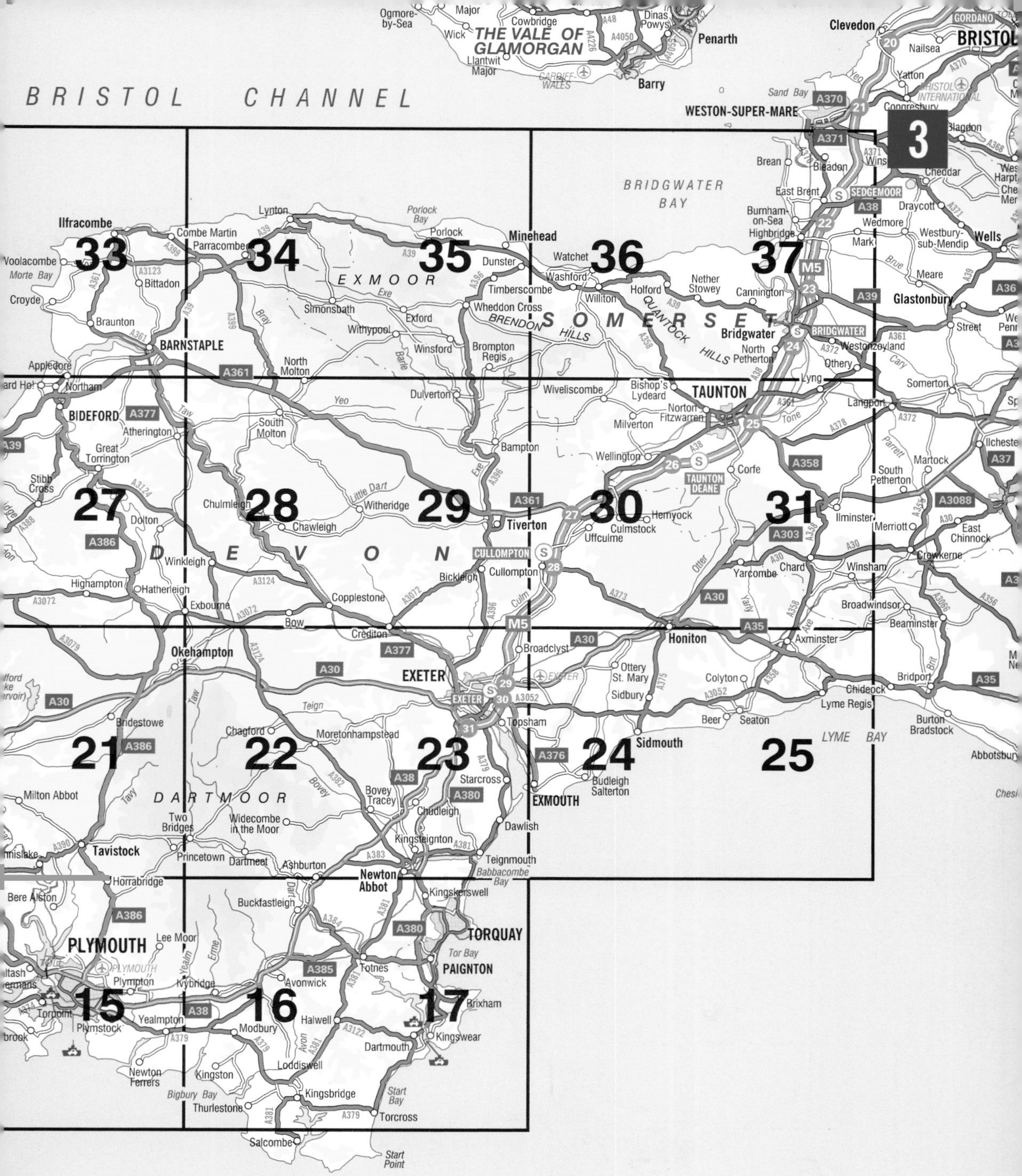

BRISTOL CHANNEL

THE VALE OF GLAMORGAN

Ogmore-by-Sea • Major • Wick • Cowbridge • Dinas Powys • Penarth
Llantwit Major • CARDIFF WALES • Barry
Clevedon • Nailsea • BRISTOL
GORDANO
Yatton • Congresbury • BRISTOL INTERNATIONAL
Sand Bay • WESTON-SUPER-MARE
3
Brean • Bleadon • Wins • Blagdon • West Harpt • Che • Mer
BRIDGWATER BAY
East Brent • Cheddar • Draycott
Burnham-on-Sea • Highbridge • SEDGEMOOR • Wedmore • Westbury-sub-Mendip
Mark • Meare • Wells
West Pen

Ilfracombe **33** • Lynton **34** • Porlock Bay • Porlock **35** • Minehead **36** • Watchet • Dunster • Washford • Timberscombe • Williton • Holford • Nether Stowey • Cannington **37** • BRIDGWATER • Glastonbury • Street

Woolacombe • Morte Bay • Croyde • Bittadon • Combe Martin • Parracombe • EXMOOR • Exe • Wheddon Cross • BRENDON HILLS • SOMERSET • QUANTOCK HILLS • North Petherton • Westonzoyland • Othery • Somerton
Braunton • BARNSTAPLE • Bray • North Molton • Withypool • Winsford • Brompton Regis • Wiveliscombe • Bishop's Lydeard • TAUNTON • Lyng • Langport

Appledore • Northam • BIDEFORD • Atherington • South Molton • Dulverton • Milverton • Norton Fitzwarren • Somerton • Ilchester
Stibb Cross • Great Torrington • Dolton **27** • Chulmleigh **28** • Witheridge • Chawleigh **29** • Bampton • Wellington • **30** Hemyock • Corfe • South Petherton **31** • Martock
DEVON • Copplestone • Tiverton • Cullompton • TAUNTON DEANE • Culmstock • Uffculme • Ilminster • Merriott • East Chinnock
Winkleigh • Hatherleigh • Exbourne • Bickleigh • Cullompton • Yarcombe • Chard • Winsham • Crewkerne
Highampton • Bow • Crediton • Broadwindsor • Beaminster

Okehampton **21** • Bridestowe • Chagford **22** • Moretonhampstead • Crediton • EXETER **23** • Broadclyst • Honiton • Axminster • Bridport **25**
Milton Abbot • Two Bridges • Widecombe in the Moor • Bovey Tracey • Chudleigh • EXETER • Topsham • Ottery St. Mary • Sidbury • Colyton • Chideock • Burton Bradstock
DARTMOOR • Princetown • Dartmeet • Ashburton • Starcross • Dawlish • EXMOUTH **24** • Sidmouth • Budleigh Salterton • Beer • Seaton • Lyme Regis • Abbotsbury
Tavistock • Horrabridge • Buckfastleigh • Kingsteignton • Teignmouth • Babbacombe Bay • LYME BAY • Chesi

PLYMOUTH • Lee Moor • Plympton • Newton Abbot • Kingskerswell • Torbay • TORQUAY
Saltash • Ivybridge • Yealmpton • Avonwick • Totnes • PAIGNTON • Brixham **17**
Torpoint • Yealmpton **15** • Modbury **16** • Halwell • Dartmouth • Kingswear
Newton Ferrers • Kingston • Loddiswell • Kingsbridge • Start Bay • Salcombe • Thurlestone • Torcross • Start Point
Bigbury Bay

MOTORWAY	**M5**
MOTORWAY UNDER CONSTRUCTION	
MOTORWAY PROPOSED	
MOTORWAY JUNCTIONS WITH NUMBERS	**22** **21**
22 Unlimited Interchange **21** Limited Interchange	
MOTORWAY SERVICE AREA	**EXETER** **S**
PRIMARY ROUTE	**A30**
MAJOR ROAD SERVICE AREAS with 24 hour Facilities Primary Route	**SALTASH** **S**
PRIMARY ROUTE DESTINATION	**EXETER**
DUAL CARRIAGEWAYS (A & B Roads)	
CLASS A ROAD, CLASS B ROAD	A396 B3181
MAJOR ROADS UNDER CONSTUCTION	
MAJOR ROADS PROPOSED	

NARROW MAJOR ROADS (Passing Places)	
GRADIENTS 1:5 (20%) and steeper	»
1:7 (14%) to 1:5 (20%)	→
TOLL	*TOLL*
MILEAGE BETWEEN MARKERS	20
RAILWAY AND STATION	*Pinhoe*
LEVEL CROSSING AND TUNNEL	
RIVER OR CANAL	*R. Yeo*
COUNTY OR UNITARY AUTHORITY BOUNDARY	
BUILT-UP AREA	
VILLAGE OR HAMLET	
WOODED AREA	
SPOT HEIGHT IN METRES	• 162
NATIONAL GRID REFERENCE (Kilometres)	3̣00
AREA COVERED BY TOWN PLANS	

TOURIST INFORMATION

AIRPORT	FOREST WALK, NATURE TRAIL	NATURAL ATTRACTION	★
AIRFIELD	FORTRESS, HILL FORT	PICNIC SITE	
HELIPORT	GARDEN (Open to Public)	PLACE OF INTEREST (General)	
ABBEY, CATHEDRAL, CHURCH, FRIARY, PRIORY (Open to Public)	GOLF COURSE ___ 9 HOLE and 18 HOLE ___	PREHISTORIC MONUMENT	
ANIMAL COLLECTION	HILL FIGURE	RAILWAY (Heritage, Narrow Gauge)	
AQUARIUM	HISTORIC BUILDING (Open to Public)	(Miniature Railway)	
ARBORETUM, BOTANICAL GARDEN	HISTORIC BUILDING & GARDEN (Open to Public)	ROMAN REMAINS	
AREA OF OUTSTANDING NATURAL BEAUTY	HORSE RACECOURSE	SANDY BEACHES	
AVIARY, BIRD GARDEN	INDUSTRIAL MONUMENT	SPOT HEIGHT (metres)	• 420
BATTLE SITE	*1643*	LEISURE PARK	TELEPHONE PUBLIC (Selected)
BRIDGE	LIGHTHOUSE	AA OR RAC	
BUTTERFLY FARM	LONG DISTANCE FOOTPATH	*S.W.C.Path*	THEME PARK
CAMPING SITE (TOURIST) (Selected)	FOOTPATH	TOURIST INFORMATION CENTRE	
CARAVAN SITE (TOURIST) (Selected)	MINE, CAVE	(All year)	
CASTLE (Open to Public)	MONUMENT, FOLLY	(Summer Season Only)	
CASTLE & GARDEN (Open to Public)	MOTOR RACING CIRCUIT	VIEWPOINT ___ 180° and 360°	
COUNTRY PARK	MUSEUM, ART GALLERY	VINEYARD, CIDERMAKER, DISTILLERY	
EARTHWORK	NATIONAL PARK , FOREST PARK	VISITOR / INFORMATION CENTRE	
ENGLISH HERITAGE SITE	NATIONAL TRUST PROPERTY	National Park	NP
FARM PARK, WORKING FARM	Always Open	*NT*	National Trust	NT
	Restricted Opening	*NT*	WILDLIFE PARK
FERRY (Vehicular)		WINDMILL	
(Foot)	NATURE RESERVE, BIRD SANCTUARY (English Nature, RSPB, selected only)	ZOO, SAFARI PARK	

1: 158,400	SCALE	2.5 Miles to 1 inch 1.584 Kms (0.98 Miles) to 1 cm

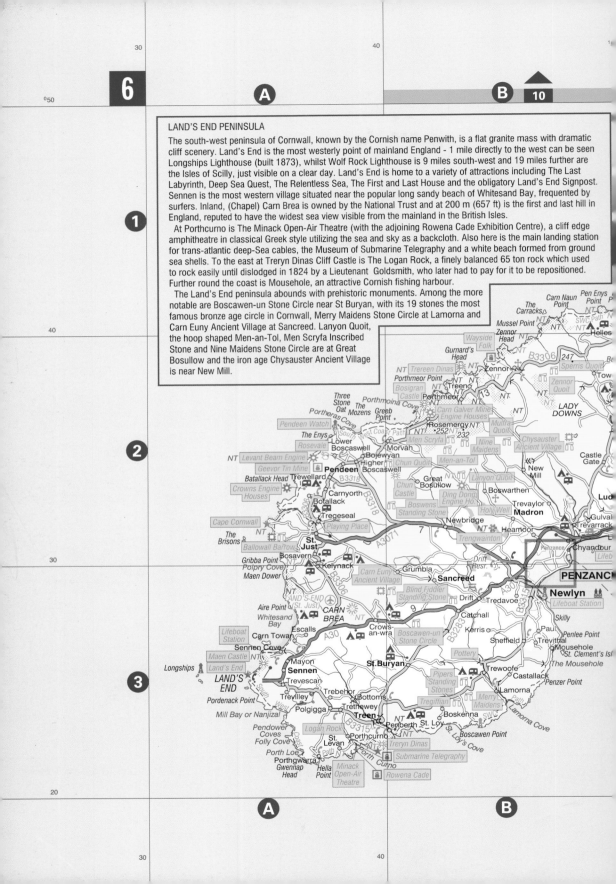

LAND'S END PENINSULA

The south-west peninsula of Cornwall, known by the Cornish name Penwith, is a flat granite mass with dramatic cliff scenery. Land's End is the most westerly point of mainland England - 1 mile directly to the west can be seen Longships Lighthouse (built 1873), whilst Wolf Rock Lighthouse is 9 miles south-west and 19 miles further are the Isles of Scilly, just visible on a clear day. Land's End is home to a variety of attractions including The Last Labyrinth, Deep Sea Quest, The Relentless Sea, The First and Last House and the obligatory Land's End Signpost. Sennen is the most western village situated near the popular long sandy beach of Whitesand Bay, frequented by surfers. Inland, (Chapel) Carn Brea is owned by the National Trust and at 200 m (657 ft) is the first and last hill in England, reputed to have the widest sea view visible from the mainland in the British Isles.

At Porthcurno is The Minack Open-Air Theatre (with the adjoining Rowena Cade Exhibition Centre), a cliff edge amphitheatre in classical Greek style utilizing the sea and sky as a backcloth. Also here is the main landing station for trans-atlantic deep-Sea cables, the Museum of Submarine Telegraphy and a white beach formed from ground sea shells. To the east at Treryn Dinas Cliff Castle is The Logan Rock, a finely balanced 65 ton rock which used to rock easily until dislodged in 1824 by a Lieutenant Goldsmith, who later had to pay for it to be repositioned. Further round the coast is Mousehole, an attractive Cornish fishing harbour.

The Land's End peninsula abounds with prehistoric monuments. Among the more notable are Boscawen-un Stone Circle near St Buryan, with its 19 stones the most famous bronze age circle in Cornwall, Merry Maidens Stone Circle at Lamorna and Carn Euny Ancient Village at Sancreed. Lanyon Quoit, the hoop shaped Men-an-Tol, Men Scryfa Inscribed Stone and Nine Maidens Stone Circle are at Great Bosullow and the iron age Chysauster Ancient Village is near New Mill.

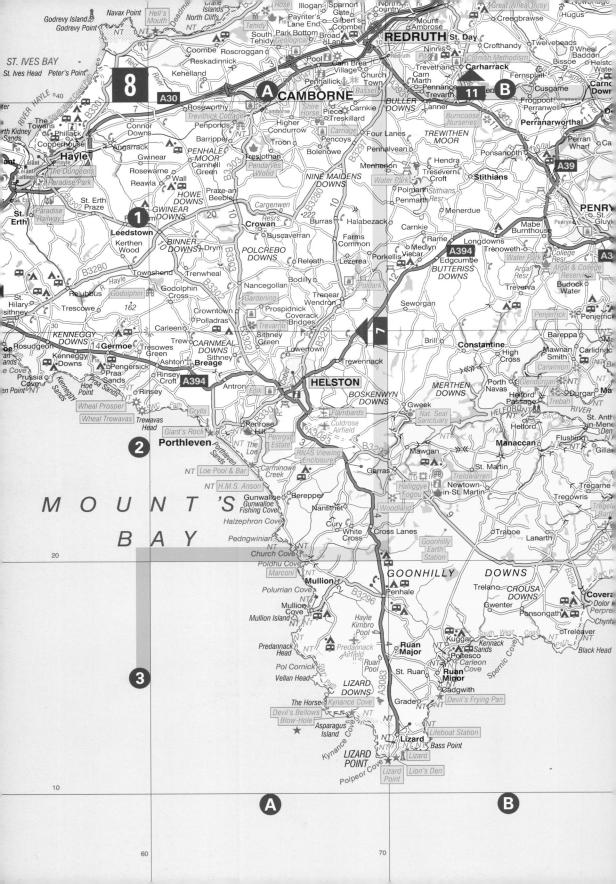

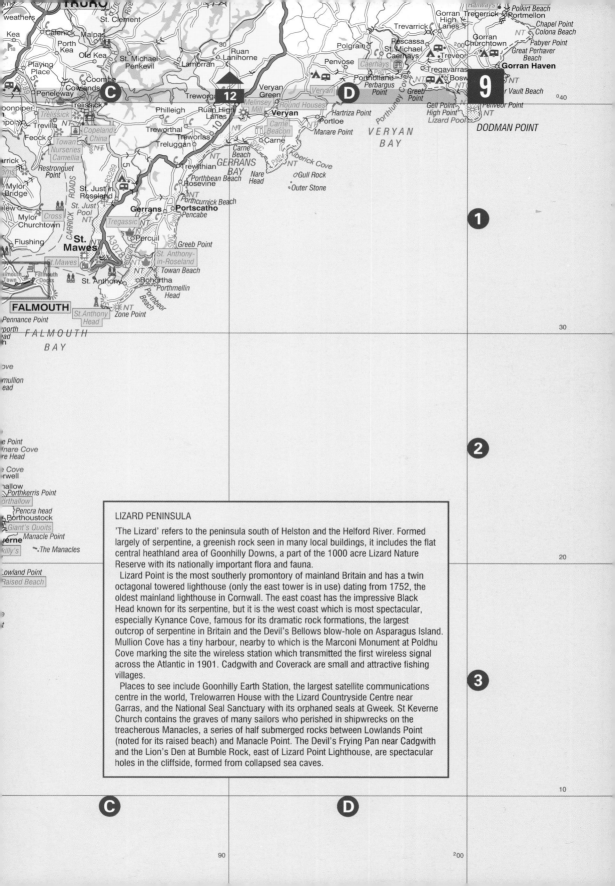

LIZARD PENINSULA

'The Lizard' refers to the peninsula south of Helston and the Helford River. Formed largely of serpentine, a greenish rock seen in many local buildings, it includes the flat central heathland area of Goonhilly Downs, a part of the 1000 acre Lizard Nature Reserve with its nationally important flora and fauna.

Lizard Point is the most southerly promontory of mainland Britain and has a twin octagonal towered lighthouse (only the east tower is in use) dating from 1752, the oldest mainland lighthouse in Cornwall. The east coast has the impressive Black Head known for its serpentine, but it is the west coast which is most spectacular, especially Kynance Cove, famous for its dramatic rock formations, the largest outcrop of serpentine in Britain and the Devil's Bellows blow-hole on Asparagus Island. Mullion Cove has a tiny harbour, nearby to which is the Marconi Monument at Poldhu Cove marking the site the wireless station which transmitted the first wireless signal across the Atlantic in 1901. Cadgwith and Coverack are small and attractive fishing villages.

Places to see include Goonhilly Earth Station, the largest satellite communications centre in the world, Trelowarren House with the Lizard Countryside Centre near Garras, and the National Seal Sanctuary with its orphaned seals at Gweek. St Keverne Church contains the graves of many sailors who perished in shipwrecks on the treacherous Manacles, a series of half submerged rocks between Lowlands Point (noted for its raised beach) and Manacle Point. The Devil's Frying Pan near Cadgwith and the Lion's Den at Bumble Rock, east of Lizard Point Lighthouse, are spectacular holes in the cliffside, formed from collapsed sea caves.

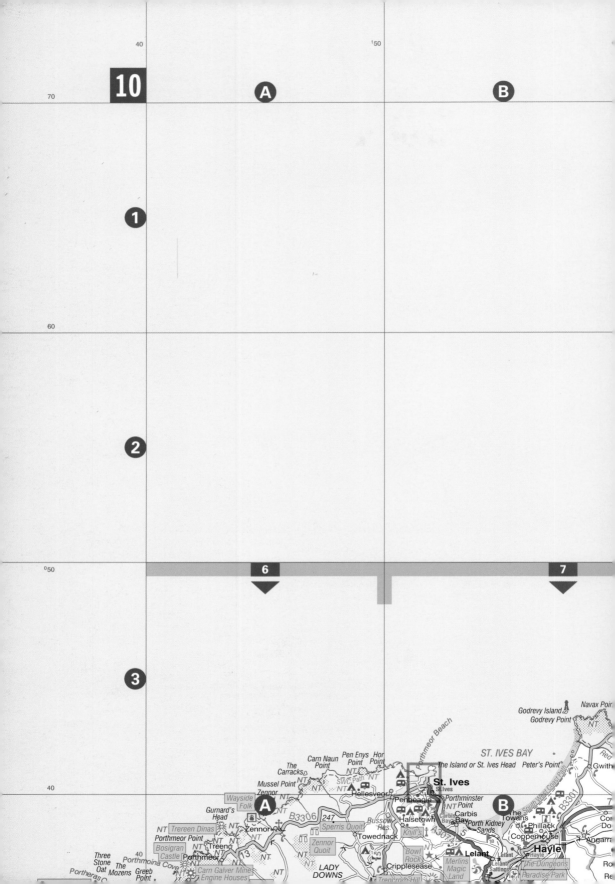

1

60

2

⁰50   6   7

3

Godrevy Island   Navax Poir
Godrevy Point
NT

Porthmeor Beach

ST. IVES BAY   Red
Carn Naun   Pen Enys Hor   The Island or St. Ives Head   Peter's Point   Gwith
Point   Point   Point
The Carracks   NT   NT
NT   NT   St Ives
Mussel Point   SWC Path   St. Ives
Zennor   NT   NT   Hellesveor   NT   Porthminster
Wayside   Point
Folk   NT   Penbeagle   NT
Gurnard's   A   B3306   247   Halsetown   Carbis   Porth Kidney   The   B3301
Head   Sperris Quoit   Bay   Sands   B   Towans   Phillack
NT   Treween Dinas   NT   NT   Bussow   Carbis   Copperhouse   Con
Porthmeor Point   Zennor   Res.   Bay   Angarr
Bosigran   NT   Treen   Zennor   Towednack   B3074   Hayle   Hayle   Ro
Castle   Porthmeor   Quoit   Lelant
Three   40   13   150   Bowl   Lelant   The Dungeons
Stone   Carn Galver Mine   Rock   Merlins   Saltings   Paradise Park
Oat   Mozens   Greeb   Engine Houses   NT   LADY   Cripplesease   Magic   Lelant   Re
Portheras   The   Point   NT   DOWNS   Land   Trencrom Hill
Porthmoina Cove

11
70
80
C
D
1
2
3
7
8
12
Treyarnon
Fox Cove
Porthcothan Bay
Porthcothan
High Cove
Park Head
Bedruthan Steps
NT
B3276
High Cove
Trenance Point
Trenance
Mawgan Porth
Berryl's Point
Beacon Cove
Trevarrian
Strasse Cliff
Watergate Bay
SWC Path
NEWQUAY (St. Mawgan)
Zacry's Island
Trevelgue Head
Towan Head
Newquay Bay
Porth
St. Columb Minor
NEWQUAY
Newquay
Pentire Point East
Pentire
Pentire Point West
West Pentire
Kelsey Head
A3058
Trencreek
Chapel
Quintrell Downs
Lane
Crantock
A392
Trevemper
Quintrell Downs
Holywell Bay
Trevowah
Carter's or Gull Rocks
Penhale Point
Fun Park
Holywell
Gannel
Gwills
Kestle
Trerice
Lawnmower
Hoblyn's Cove
Ligger Point
Tresean
Treveal
Penhale Camp
Cubert
B3075
Trevoll
Benny Halt
Benny Mill
Penhale Sands
Perran Beach
Ligger or Perran Bay
St. Piran's Oratory
St. Newlyn East
Rejerrah
Lappa Valley Steam Railway
Trevilson
East Wheal Rose
Lappa Valley
Gear Sands
Treamble
Newlyn Halt
Fiddlers Green
Cotty's Point
Rose
St. Piran's
Shepherds
NEWLYN DOWNS
Perranzabuloe Folk
Perranporth
Cligga Head
Goonhavern
B3285
A39
Bawden Rocks or Man & his man
B3284
Bolingey
Perrancoombe
Lifeboat Station
Perranporth
Cocks
Perranwell
World in Miniature
Newdowns Head
Trevellas
Penwartha
Zelah
Crams
Cross Coombe
Blue Hills Tin Streams
Perranzabuloe
Wheal Frances
ST.AGNES HEAD
Higher Bal
Barkla Shop
Blowinghouse
Ventongimps
Mithian
Penhallow
St. Allen
Tubby's Head
St. Agnes
A3075
Callestick
Marazanvose
Trispen
Wheal Cotes Engine House
Cider Farm
St. Erme
Chapel Porth
Goonvrea
Goonbell
Tresawsen
Mingoose
Towan Cross
Coldharbour
Allet
Idless Wood
Porth Towan
B3277
Silverwell
Porthtowan
Mount Hawke
A30
Little Croft West
Shortlanesend
Idless
Sheep Rock
Two Burrows
Three Burrows
Roseworthy
Menagissey
ATV Centre
Tramroads
Skinner's Bottom
Buckshead
Gull Rock
Airfield (Disused)
Blackwater
Langarth
Kenwyn
Ralph's Cupboard
Portreath
Cambrose
Mawla Forge
Green Bottom
A390
New Mill
Deadman's Cove
Samphire Island
B3300
B3301
Goldsmiths
Wheal Rose
NORTH DOWNS
Chacewater
Threemilestone
Truro
TRURO
Crane Islands
North Cliffs
Bridge
Rose
Illogan
Sparnon Gate
Scorrier
Great Wheal Busy
Newbridge
Higher-town
Tehidy
Paynter's Lane End
North Country
Hugus
Penweathers
St. Clement
Gilbert's Coombe
Mount Ambrose
Creegbrawse
South Tehidy
Park Bottom
Geological
Broad Lane
REDRUTH
St. Day
Kea
Calenick
Malpas
Porth Kea
Coombe
Roscroggan
Crofthandy
Twelveheads
Wheal Baddon
Old Kea
Reskadinnick
Pool
Carn Brea Village
Ninnis
Pit
Cornish Methodism
Bissoe
Helston Water
Playing Place
Kehelland
Church Town
Trevethan
Carharrack
Fernsplatt
Carnon
Coombe
Penhallick
A3047
Carn Marth
B3298
Carnon Downs
Cowlands
A30
CAMBORNE
Basset
A393
Pennance
Gwennap
Cusgarne
Peneleway
Trevarth
Frogpool
Perranwell
Trelissick
Roseworthy
Shire Horse
Piece
Carnkie
BULLER DOWNS
Lanner
Perranwell
Devoran
Goonpiper
Trevithick Cottage
Treskillard
Burncoose
Perranarworthal
Penpol
Trevilla
Copeland China
Penponds
Higher Condurrow
Carriage
Four Lanes
TREWITHEN MOOR
Feock
Towan Nurseries Camellia
Barripper
Troon
Pencoys
Burncoose Nurseries
Perran Wharf
Carclew
PENHALE MOOR
Bolenowe
Penhalvean
Kennall
Ponsanooth
Restronguet Point
Carnhell Green
Treslothan
B3297
Angarrick
Pendarves Wood
Menherion
Hendra
A39
Lanterns
B3303
Wall
NINE MAIDENS DOWNS
Water Park
Tresevern Croft
Stithians
B3289

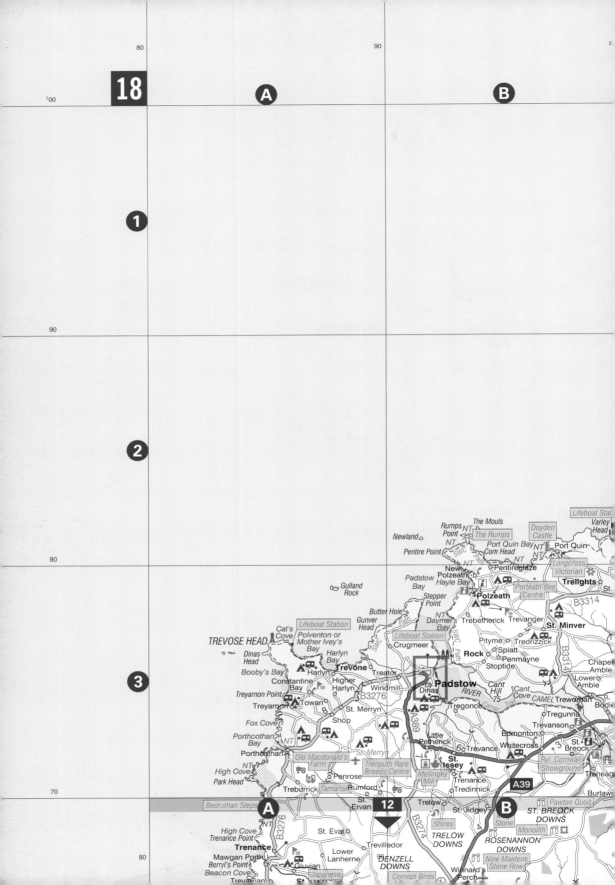

BUDE
BAY

CORNWALL

DEVON

1

2

3

A

B

20

Hartland
POINT

Barley
Bay

Shipload
Bay

Chapman
Rock

NT

Beckland
Bay

Windbury Point

Blackchurch Rock

South West Coast Path

Titchberry

Exmansworthy

Damehole
Point

Hartland
Abbey

Abbey River

Norton

Velly

Wood Rock

Gallant Rock

Clovelly

Bight a
Doubleyou

Babbacombe Mouth
Babbacombe Cliff
Higher Rowden

Gauter
Point

Hartland
Quay

St. Catherine's Tor

Hartland
Quay

Stoke

Hartland

Rosedown

Higher
Clovelly

Lifeboat

Fisherman's Cottage

The
Kingsley

Hobby Drive

Buck's
Mills

Horns
Cross

Cornbo

Speke's Mill
Mouth Waterfall

Speke's Mill
Mouth

Longpeak

Milford

Docton
Mill.

Natcott

Clovelly
Dykes

North
Devon

The
Milky Way

The
Lynbarn
Railway

Buck's
Cross

Waytown

Goldworthy

Elmscott

Edistone

Philham

Welsford

West
Town

Cranford

Woolfardisworthy
or Woolsery

Parkham

Parkham
Ash

Gull Rock

Embury
Beach

South
Hole

Lutsford

Huddisford

Alminstone
Cross

Melbury
Resr.

Lower
Twitchen

Knaps Longpeak

Welcome Mouth

Welcombe

Darracott

Meddon

Ashmansworthy

Dipple

East
Putford

Marsland Mouth

Mead

Marsland Water

Woolley

Gull Rock

Yeol Mouth

Gooseham

Eastcott

West
Youlstone

East
Youlstone

Dinworthy

Gnome
Reserve

West
Putford

Colscott

Haytown

Lucky Hole

Morwenstow

Crimp

Killarney
Springs

River Waldon

Torridge

Bu

Higher Sharpnose
Point

Hawker's
Hut

Shop

Woodford

Bradworthy

Stanbury Mouth

Lower Sharpnose
Point

Pixieland
Fun Park

Kilkhampton

Lamberal Water

Upper Tamar Lake

Tamar Lakes
Water Park

Lower Tamar
Lake

Alfardisworthy

Sutcombe

Brendon

Abbots
Bickington

Steeple Point

Coombe
Valley

NT

Pixieland

Thurdon

Sutcombemill

River Waldon

Shop

Coombe

Duckpool

NT

Kilkhampton

Thorne

Forda

Tamar Lakes

Soldon
Cross

Venngreen

Milton
Damerel

Sandy Mouth

Stibb

A39

B3254

River Neet

Woodsdown
Hill

Holsworthy
Beacon

Woodacott

Long Rock

Menachurch Point

Northcott Mouth

Maer

Poughill

Hersham

Dexbeer

Lana

Thorne
Farm

Chilsworthy

Wo
Cro

Bush

Spell Brook

Flexbury

Crooklets Beach
Bude Haven

1643

STRATTON

Grimscott

Holsworthy
Woods

Cookbury
Wick

Lynstone

BUDE

Red
Post

Launcells
Cross

A3072

Pancrasweek

HOLSWORTHY

Derriton
Pyworthy

Staddon

Anvil
Corner

Phillip's Point

Upton

Thorne

Inclined
Plane

Chasty

Whimble

Simpson
Farm

Higher Longbeak

Marhamchurch

Borough

Churchtown

Bridgerule

Leworthy

Hollacombe

Lower Longbeak

Widemouth
Bay

Titson

Merrifield

Black Rock

Wanson Mouth

Box's
Shop

Langford
Barton

A388

Clawford

Millook Haven

Cancleave

Dizzard
Point

Millook

Coppathorne

Treskinnick
Cross

B3254

Claw

Chipman
Strand

NT

Poundstock

NT

Thorn's
Beach

NT

Treworgie
Barton

Dizzard

Tregole

Trewint

Penhallam

The College

Whitstone

Tamar

North
Tamerton

Blagdon Fa

St Gennys

A39

Week Green

Week
St. Mary

Street

Telcott

Blagdon

B. Claw

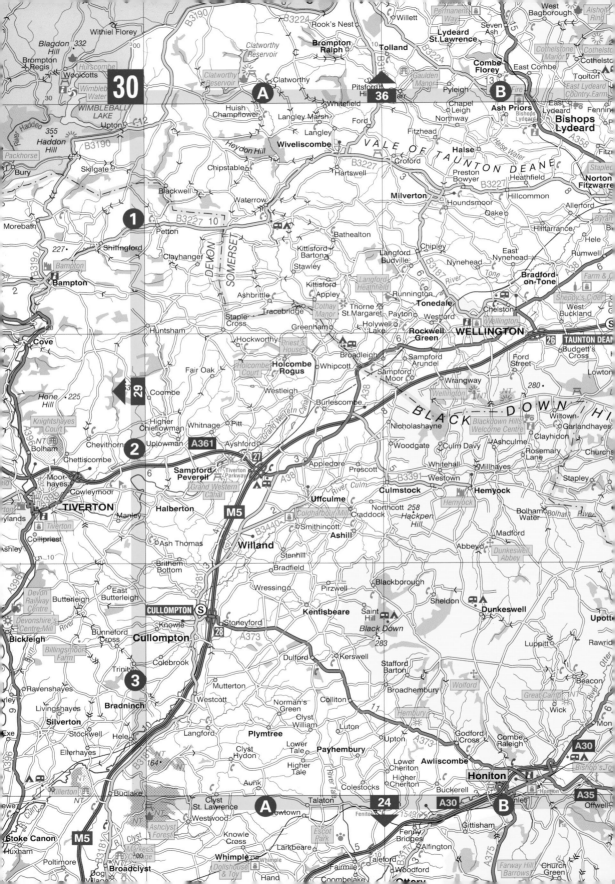

20
30

60

1

LUNDY

Lundy lies in the Bristol Channel 12 miles north west of Hartland Point. 3 miles long by between 0.25 and 0.75 miles wide and rising to over 130 m (427 ft), the island is almost completely made of light coloured granite covered in grass and heather. The west and south coasts are the finest with tall cliffs providing tremendous views over the 4,000 miles of the Atlantic, whilst the east and north coasts give views to the Devon coast and South Wales. The sea around Lundy is a designated Marine Nature Reserve noted for seals and famous for puffins.

Lundy was held by the piratical de Marisco family in the 13th century and later by the Royalists in the Civil War, the present castle being rebuilt during this time. There are three lighthouses, the Old Light of 1820 on Beacon Hill (the highest point of the island), designed by the architect of Dartmoor prison, was often obscured by mist and was replaced by the North and South Lights in 1897, both currently in use. Also of note are the Devil's Slide, a spectacular granite slab sloping into the sea on the west coast and the Devil's Limekiln, a deep hole at Shutter Point.

Lundy is owned by the National Trust but administered by the Landmark Trust who acquired the island in 1969. It has around twenty residents, a church, tavern and shop, but no cars. The MS Oldenburg sails to the island from Bideford (2.25 hours) all year, and Ilfracombe (2.25 hours) and Clovelly (1.5 hours, less frequently) between April and October. Landing is by launch to the beach. Day trips, camping and longer stays in self catering accommodation are possible.

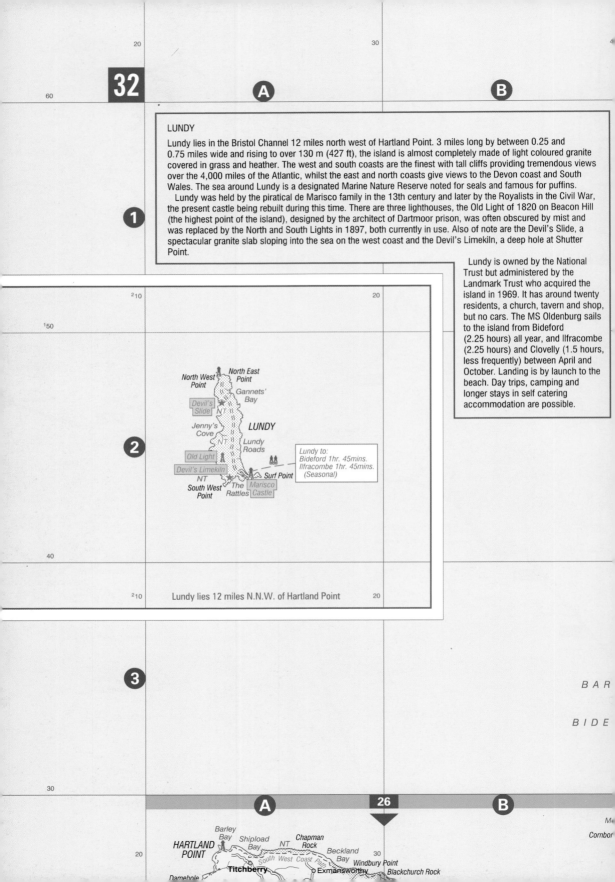

²10   20

¹50

2

North West Point — North East Point
Gannets' Bay
Devil's Slide   NT
Jenny's Cove
NT   Lundy Roads
LUNDY
Old Light
Devil's Limekiln
NT   Surf Point
South West Point   The Rattles   Marisco Castle

Lundy to:
Bideford 1hr. 45mins.
Ilfracombe 1hr. 45mins.
(Seasonal)

40

²10   Lundy lies 12 miles N.N.W. of Hartland Point   20

3

B A R
B I D E

Barley Bay
Shipload Bay   Chapman Rock
HARTLAND POINT   NT   Beckland Bay
South West Coast Path   Windbury Point
Titchberry   Exmansworthy   Blackchurch Rock
Damehole

20   30

Me
Cornbor

1

ILFRACOMBE

Ilfracombe to
Lundy 1hr. 45mins.
(Seasonal)

Bull Point
Rockham
Bay
Morte
Point **Mortehoe**
Grunta Beach
Grunta Pool
Barricane Beach
Woolacombe
Baggy Point
Croyde Bay
Croyde
Croyde Bay

Shag
Point
Flat
Point
Lee   Higher
Slade   Hillsborough
Gate House   Lower
Slade   Chambercombe
Heritage   Miniature Ponies &
Centre   Shire Horse Centre
Once Upon   Mullacott
a Time   Mullacott Cross
Borough
Cross
Two
Pots
Trimstone
Cheglinch
**West
Down**
Willingcott
Chapel Wood
Dean
Cross
North
Buckland
Gem, Rock & Shell
Georgeham
Forda
Darracott
Cross
Winsham
Knowle
B3231   Lobb
Halsinger
Boode
Saunton
Pippacott
Whitehall
Saunton Sands
Braunton
Braunton
Great Field
Velator
Wrafton
Elliott Gallery
Heanton
Punchardon
The
Butterfly
House
Chivenor
Tarka
Ashford
Ashford
Braunton
Burrows
Tarka
Trail
Taw Torridge
Pottington
Isley Marshes
Tarka
Trail
Fremington
Muddlebridge
Bickington
Lifeboat
Station
North Devon
Maritime
Yelland
Brannams Pottery
Lake
Worlington
Bickleton
Brynsworthy
Northam
Burrows
Signal Box
Instow
Tapeley
Park
Appledore
Pebble
Ridge
Marshford
Organic
Westward Ho!
Rock Nose
id's Pool
Path
Range
B3236
Buckleigh
Silford
Raleigh Hill
Northam
Westleigh
Holmacott
St. John's
Chapel
Easta
Horwood
Eastleigh
Lower
Lovacott
Abbotsham
The Big
Sheep
BIDEFORD
Orchard
Burton
Art Gallery
Chudleigh Fort
**East-the-
Water**
Woodtown
Stony
**Newton
Tracey**
Harracott
Chapelton
Herner
Week

Hele
Bay   Rillage
Point   Widmouth
Head   Combe
Martin
Bay   Hangman
Point   Blackstone
Point   The Mare
& Colt   Highve
Poin
Old Corn
Mill   Widmouth   Little
Hangman   Elwill
Bay   Heddon's
Cleave & Mouth
Watermouth
Castle   S.W. Coast Path   Trentishoe
Goosewell   Motorcycle   Blackstone Down   NT 349   Kema
Haggington
Hill   **Combe
Martin**   NT   Heale
A399   Combe
Martin   **34**   Killi
Chambercombe
Manor   **Berrynarbor**   Pack O'
Cards Inn   Dean   **Parra**
Combe   Holwell Ca
Henstridge   Martin   **2**   Kentisbury   A399
Berry Down   Kentisbury   337
Cross   Ford   **Black**
A3123   269   7   Patchole
East   Wistlandpound
Down   Reservoir
Bittadon   Indicott   Clifton   Arlington   Exmoor
Churchill   Beccott   40
B3230   258   Arlington
Middle   Arlington   Knightacott   Fou
Marwood   Milltown   Court   Cros
NT   Wa
Muddiford   Loxhore   261
Marwood   Higher
Hill   Muddiford   Lower   **Bratton
Fleming**
Marwood   Guineaford   Loxhore
Prixford   **Shirwell**
A39   Stoke
Snapper   **Hakeford**   Rivers
Ashford   Bradford   **3**   rtleigh   Gunn   Accott   Sto
Sticklepath   **BARNSTAPLE**   **Goodleigh**   229   Stoodleig
Fort Hill   Jungleland   Bradninch
Newport   A361
Landkey   Riverton
Rumsam   Landkey   **Swimbridge**
Gatehouse   Newland   Swimbridge   Tordown
North Devon   Newland
**Bishop's
Tawstock   Tawton**   Hannaford   **Swimbridge**
A377   Cobbaton   East
Combat   Stowford
Collection   Stowford

B3230

Bideford to
Lundy 1hr. 45mins.

STAPLE
OR
RD BAY

RIVER TAW

Woolacombe Sand

A3123

B3343

B3233

RIVER TORRIDGE

A39

A361

A399

A3229

B3232

C   90   D   300   60

1

150

36

MINEHEAD

West Somerset Railway

Yellow Stone
Ivy Stone
Porlock Weir Scenic Toll Road
Hurlstone Point
Selworthy Sand
Minehead Bluff
Burgundy Chapel
Greenaleigh Point
North Hill

thorne tum
Gore Point
Porlock Bay
Porlock Weir
Bossington
Bossington Farm
Coast Path
BLUE ANCHOR BAY

Culbone
moor Natural story Centre
TOLL
Porlock
Lynch
Allerford
Selworthy
Woodcombe
Higher Town
Minehead
2
Home Farm

y Gate
Oare
West Porlock
Porlock Scenic Toll Road
Piles Watermill
Periton
Yarn Market
Dunster
Marsh Street
6

Robber's
436
Whit Stones
Hawkcombe
A39
Horner Wood
Tivington
Alcombe
Butter Cross
Dovecote
Dunster
Great Western Railway
Chapel Cleeve
B3191

Oareford
Porlock Stone Circle
413
Horner
Luccombe
Cloutsham
Wootton Courtenay
River Avill
Gallox
NT
Dunster
Blue Anchor
Old Cleeve
Kentsford House

one alley
Outer Alscott
Horner Wood
Stoke Pero
Huntscott
Burrow
Carhampton
Bat's Castle
A39
Washford
Cleeve

T
Dunkery Hill
519 NT
Joaney How & Robin How Burial Cairns
Timberscombe
Nutcombe Bottom
Withycombe
Bilbrook
Washford
S&DR
Torre Cider

Alderman's Barrow
Dunkery Beacon
A396
Monkham Hill
381
Hungerford
Rodhuish
Torre Cider
Lower Roadwater
Beggearn Huish

M   O   O   R
Newland
Edgcott
B3224
6
Wheddon Cross
Cutcombe
Kersham Hill
361
Luxborough
Kingsbridge
Roadwater
B3190
Com Syden

3223
4
Exford
Luckwell Bridge
386
B3223
River Exe
Packhorse
River Quarme
B   R   E   N   D   O   N
Treborough
Leighland Chapel
Chidgley

Landacre
NATIONAL
Winsford Hill
426
Winsford
Gupworthy
H   I   L   L   S

Withypool
428 Withypool Common
Wambarrows NT
Caratacus Stone
Week
Exton
Bridgetown
3
Withiel Florey
B3190

PARK
Liscombe
South Hill
361
A396
Blagdon Hill
332
Hurscombe
Clatworthy Reservoir

SOMERSET
DEVON
Tarr Steps
Brompton Regis
Woolcotts
Clatworthy Reservoir
Cla

77
Round Hill
Hancock Stone
Hawkridge
Wimbleball Lake Water Park
WIMBLEBALL LAKE

lland
C
West Anstey Common
29
D
Upton
A
Huish Champflower
La

301
West Anstey
Guildhall Heritage Centre
NP Castle
Dulverton
Haddon Hill
355
B3190
Heydon Hill

Lee
Battleton
B3222
B3223
Packhorse
River Barle
Bury
Skilgate
Chipstable

Xoo Mill
East
300

TOWN PLANS

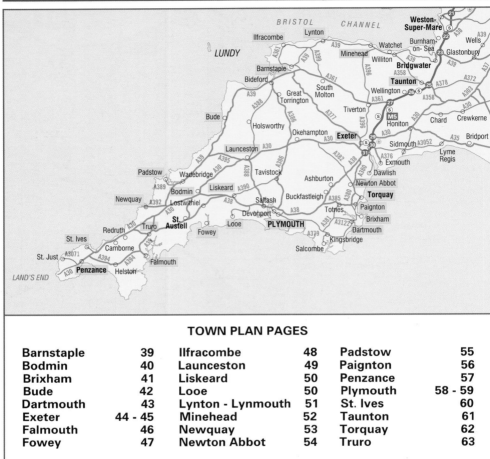

TOWN PLAN PAGES

TOWN PLAN ONLY SYMBOLS

SEE PAGE 5 FOR COMPLETE MAP AND TOURIST REFERENCES

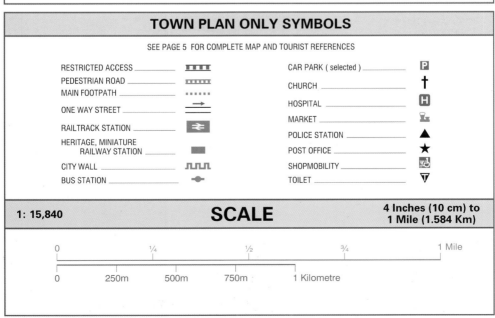

RESTRICTED ACCESS	▮▮▮▮	CAR PARK (selected)	🅿
PEDESTRIAN ROAD	▪▪▪▪▪▪	CHURCH	†
MAIN FOOTPATH	▪ ▪ ▪ ▪		
ONE WAY STREET	→	HOSPITAL	🄷
RAILTRACK STATION	🚆	MARKET	
HERITAGE, MINIATURE RAILWAY STATION	▬	POLICE STATION	▲
		POST OFFICE	★
CITY WALL	⌐⌐⌐⌐	SHOPMOBILITY	
BUS STATION	⊶	TOILET	▽

1: 15,840	# SCALE	**4 Inches (10 cm) to 1 Mile (1.584 Km)**

0 ¼ ½ ¾ 1 Mile

0 250m 500m 750m 1 Kilometre

Barnstaple is a market town and former port situated on the tidal River Taw where it is crossed by the widened 13th century sixteen arch Long Bridge. The town traded in Barum ware pottery and this is still made at Brannams Pottery (on Roundswell Industrial Estate to the south west). There is a Pannier Market in the large Market House on Butchers Row and on Paternoster Row nearby is St Anne's Chapel, an early chantry chapel once used as a grammar school. A pleasant riverside walk runs along the quay, off The Strand, leading to Queen Anne's Walk, a colonnaded arcade of 1796 with a statue of Queen Anne.

PLACES OF INTEREST

Tourist Information Centre (All year) - 36 Boutport Street.
Tel: 01271 375000

◆ BARNSTAPLE CASTLE- Mound & traces of a moat of the former Norman castle. Tuly Street. ◆ BARNSTAPLE HERITAGE CENTRE - Displays on history of Barnstaple. Queen Anne's Walk, The Strand. ◆ NORTH DEVON, THE MUSEUM OF (MUSEUM ON THE SQUARE) - Pottery industry, Royal North Devon Yeomanry, Tarka Centre with natural history of otters. North Devon Athenaeum, The Square. ◆ TARKA TRAIL - 180 mile footpath. 29.5 miles from Braunton through Barnstaple & Bideford to Meeth are a cycleway on the former Southern Railway line. ◆ TAW TORRIDGE COUNTRY PARK - 8.5 mile linear country park between Barnstaple & Bideford on former Southern Railway line. Part of the Tarka Trail (see above) & the South West Coast Path.

ENTERTAINMENT

◆ Cinemas - Boutport Street.
◆ Theatres - Queens Theatre, Boutport Street.

SPORT & LEISURE

◆ Parks & Gardens - Castle Mound, Tuly Street. Pilton Park, Pilton Causeway. Rock Park, New Road.
◆ Sports Centres - North Devon Leisure Centre, Seven Brethren Bank, Sticklepath. Park School Community Sports Hall, Park Lane (SE Barnstaple).
◆ Swimming Pools - North Devon Leisure Centre (as above).
◆ Ten-Pin Bowling - Lets Go Superbowl, Braunton Road.

Hartland Point

Clovelly

BODMIN

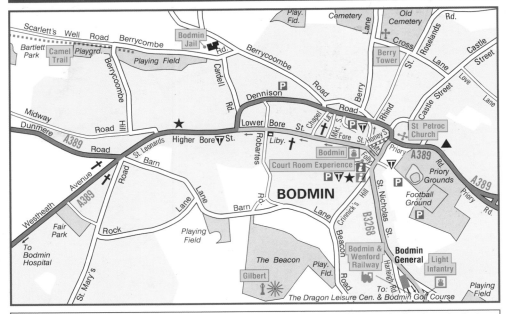

Bodmin, situated on a hillside site, is the former county town of Cornwall. The town had an important priory until the Dissolution. Of note are the neo-classical granite Shire Hall (the former County Assize Court building of 1838 on Mount Folly last used in 1988 - see below), the county prison and St Petroc's Church (see below). The Beacon has panoramic views.

PLACES OF INTEREST
Tourist Information Centre (All year)- The Shire Hall, Mount Folly. Tel: 01208 76616
◆ BERRY TOWER - Remains of tower of St Annes Priory. Old Cemetery, Berry Lane. ◆ BODMIN & WENFORD RAILWAY - 6 mile standard gauge steam railway. Stations at Bodmin General, Colesloggett Halt (for Cardinham Woods), Bodmin Parkway (main line) & Boscarne Junction (for Camel Trail). Bodmin General Station, Lostwithiel Road. ◆ BODMIN JAIL - Former county prison dating back to 1776. Exhibition with recreated displays in dungeons & cells. Berrycombe Road. ◆ BODMIN MUSEUM - History of Bodmin up to the end of WWII. Costumes, domestic and farming artifacts. Mount Folly. ◆ CAMEL TRAIL - Popular 17 mile cycleway & footpath on former LSWR railway line linking Padstow, Wadebridge & Bodmin, continuing to Poley's Bridge nr. Wenfordbridge. ◆ DUKE OF CORNWALL'S LIGHT INFANTRY MUSEUM - Regimental history, military artefacts, uniforms & medals. The Keep, Victoria Barracks, Plas Newydd Avenue. ◆ GILBERT MONUMENT - 44 m (144 ft) high granite obelisk in memory of Sir Walter Raleigh Gilbert. The Beacon. ◆ ST PETROC CHURCH - Cornwall's largest church containing 12th century reliquary of St Petroc. Priory Road. ◆ SHIRE HALL COURT ROOM EXPERIENCE - Recreation of the 19th century trial, in original court building, of murderer of Charlotte Dymond whose body was found on Rough Tor in 1844. Holding cells. The Shire Hall, Mount Folly. ◆ TOWN & COUNTRYSIDE CENTRE - History, wildlife, information on Camel trail, activities, places to see in Bodmin, on Bodmin Moor & in the surrounding area. The Shire Hall, Mount Folly.

SPORT & LEISURE
◆ Parks & Gardens - Fair Park, Westheath Avenue. Priory Ground, Priory Road. The Beacon, Beacon Rd.
◆ Sports Centres - The Dragon Leisure Centre, Lostwithiel Road (S of Bodmin General Station).
◆ Swimming Pools - The Dragon Leisure Centre (as above).

Cornish Countryside

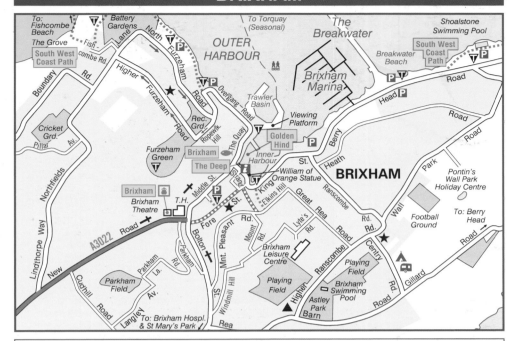

Brixham, a popular small fishing port with narrow streets, was described in 1850 as 'the largest fishery in England' and it is still an important trawler port with a busy fish market. The half mile long breakwater protects the outer harbour and Brixham Marina whilst a viewing platform on the New Pier (built in 1803/4), accessible to the public, overlooks the Trawler Basin. A statue on the Strand commemorates William of Orange's landing in Brixham in 1688 and preserved WWII gun battery emplacements can be seen in Battery Gardens.

PLACES OF INTEREST
Tourist Information Centre (All year)- The Old Market House, The Quay. Tel: 01803 852861
◆ BRIXHAM AQUARIUM - Marine life including sharks, octopi & eels. 12 The Quay. ◆ BRIXHAM MUSEUM - Local & maritime history including shipbuilding, smuggling, lifeboats, the coastguard, trawler models, pictures & costume. Bolton Cross, New Road. ◆ GOLDEN HIND, THE - Replica of Sir Francis Drake's ship on which he sailed around the world in 1577-80. Displays on life at sea. The Quay.
◆ THE DEEP - History, fables & monsters of the ocean. Re-creations of sea cave, trawler, sunken pirate ship featuring whales, mermaids & folklore. The Old Market House, The Quay.

ENTERTAINMENT
◆ Theatres - Brixham Theatre, New Road.

SPORT & LEISURE
◆ Parks & Gardens - Astley Park, Higher Ranscombe Road.
Battery Gardens, North Furzeham Road.
Furzeham Green, Higher Furzeham Road.
Parkham Field, Parkham Lane.
St Mary's Park, Upton Manor Road (S Brixham).
◆ Sports Centres - Brixham Leisure Centre, Lyte's Road.
◆ Swimming Pools - Brixham Swimming Pool, Higher Ranscombe Road. Shoalstone Swimming Pool, Berry Head Road.

Brixham

BUDE

Bude grew up as an agricultural trading port, serving the surrounding remote rural area, to which it was linked by the 35 mile long Bude Canal built in the 1820s. Known for its inclined planes instead of locks, the 2 miles to Helebridge survive with pleasant towpath walks. Bude later became a Victorian & Edwardian resort and it remains a popular family seaside destination. Crooklets Beach is used for surfing. The Castle (now council offices) was built in 1850 by Sir Goldsworthy Gurney, best known for his invention of incandescent lighting and the steam powered road coach.

PLACES OF INTEREST

Tourist Information Centre (All year)- Bude Visitor Centre, The Crescent car park.
Tel: 01288 354240
◆ BUDE-STRATTON MUSEUM - Displays on the Bude Canal, railway & local shipwrecks. Audio-visual. Lower Wharf. ◆ BUDE VISITOR CENTRE - Information on the natural history of the Bude area. The Crescent car park. ◆ COMPASS POINT STORM TOWER - Eight sided storm tower marked with points of the compass. Compass Point, Efford Down. ◆ LIFEBOAT STATION - Established in 1837. Inflatable 'D' lifeboat. South Lock Pier, Breakwater Road.

SPORT & LEISURE

◆ Parks & Gardens - Summerleaze Down, Crooklets Road.
◆ Sports Centres - Budehaven Leisure Centre, Budehaven School, Stratton Road.
◆ Swimming Pools - Seawater Pool, Summerleaze Beach. Splash Leisure Pool, Stratton Road.

Coastline Cornwall

DARTMOUTH

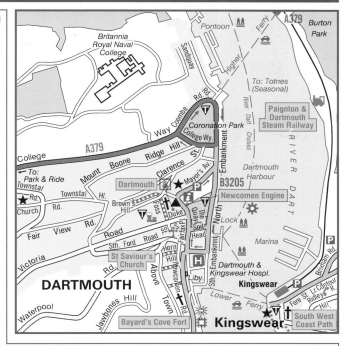

Dartmouth is an historic port and holiday centre on the west side of the beautiful land-locked estuary of the River Dart. Once important for the export of cloth and for trade with Newfoundland, the town is characterized by narrow streets, alleyways and long flights of steps such as Horn Hill and Browns Hill (once the main packhorse route). The South Embankment quay is ideal for harbour watching and from here the foot ferry crosses to Kingswear and popular river cruises leave for Totnes, 10 miles upstream, and trips past Dartmouth Castle downstream. Buildings of note include The Butterwalk in Duke Street dating from 1635-40 with elaborately carved overhanging timbers, the colonnaded Old Market House (dating from the 1830s) in Market Square and the famous Britannia Royal Naval College of 1905.

PLACES OF INTEREST

Tourist Information Centre (All year)- The Engine House, Mayor's Avenue. Tel: 01803 834224
◆ BAYARD'S COVE FORT (EH) - Small artillery fort of 1510 built to protect the harbour entrance. Riverfront, Southtown. ◆ DARTMOUTH MUSEUM - Maritime history, ship models, pictures and artifacts relating to Dartmouth & its estuary. The Butterwalk, Duke Street. ◆ NEWCOMEN MEMORIAL ENGINE - Engine of 1725, a memorial to Dartmouth born Thomas Newcomen, inventor of the atmospheric steam pumping engine. The Engine House, Royal Avenue Gardens, Mayor's Avenue. ◆ PAIGNTON & DARTMOUTH STEAM RAILWAY - 7 mile standard gauge steam railway using GWR engines. Stations at Kingswear, Churston, Goodrington, Paignton. Kingswear Station, Kingswear. ◆ ST SAVIOUR'S CHURCH - Noted for its 15th century ornate rood screen with painted panels of saints. Church Close.

SPORT & LEISURE

◆ Parks & Gardens - Coronation Park, North Embankment. Royal Avenue Gardens, Mayor's Avenue.

River Dart

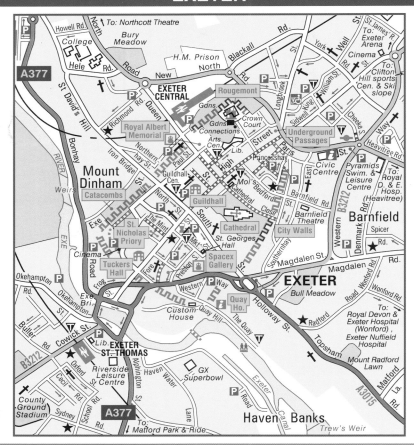

Exeter, a cathedral and university city, is the county 'town' of Devon and remains an historic city despite damage from wartime bombing raids in 1942. Of note are Fore Street, the cobbled Stepcote Hill (the only surviving medieval street in the city), Mol's Coffee House of 1596 in Cathedral Close and the Custom House of 1681 on the Quay. The city was once a major port exporting woollen cloth and is connected with the Exe estuary at Topsham by the 5 mile long Exeter Ship Canal, built in the 1560s, followed by a canalside walk. 'Exeter Historic Quayside' is now a popular waterside area with shops and restaurants.

Exeter Cathedral

Tudor Buildings, Exeter

Dart Valley

PLACES OF INTEREST

Tourist Information Centre (All year) - Civic Centre, Paris Street. Tel: 01392 265700

◆ CATACOMBS, THE - Underground catacombs of the citys 17th century old cemetery. Guided tours only (inquire at tourist information centre). Bartholomew Street East.

◆ EXETER CATHEDRAL - Symmetrical building with twin Norman towers, the peak of the Decorated Gothic style in England. Longest Gothic vaulted nave in the country. West front sculptures. Cathedral Close.

◆ EXETER CITY WALLS - Roman town wall of 200 AD rebuilt in medieval times (no gateways survive). Best sections off Southernhay West, Bartholomew Street East, Northernhay Street & Northernhay Gardens.

◆ EXETER GUILDHALL - One of the oldest municipal buildings to survive in England still in use, dating from 1330 with a pillared facade of 1593. City's silver & regalia on display. High Street.

◆ EXETER ROUGEMONT CASTLE - Early Norman gatehouse & fragments of wall remain. Crown Court of 1774 & Rougemont Gardens now occupy most of the site. Castle Street.

◆ EXETER UNDERGROUND PASSAGES - Medieval underground conduits built to supply fresh water to the city. Exhibition, audio-visual, guided tour. Britain's only subterranean waterways open to the public. Eastgate, off High Street (nr. Boots).

◆ QUAY HOUSE VISITOR CENTRE - History of the port of Exeter with models, paintings & artifacts. Audio-visual on story of Exeter from its Roman origins to the present day. 46 The Quay.

◆ ROYAL ALBERT MEMORIAL MUSEUM & ART GALLERY - Exeter silver, Devon archaeology & natural history, paintings by Devon artists, fine art, ceramics, glass. Queen Street.

◆ ST NICHOLAS PRIORY - Guest wing of an 11th century Benedictine priory with a Norman undercroft, kitchen & guest hall. The Mint, off Fore Street.

◆ SPACEX GALLERY - Changing contemporary art exhibitions. 45 Preston Street.

◆ TUCKERS HALL - Medieval guild hall of the Weavers, Fullers & Shearmen of the wool & cloth trade, with an arched braced roof of 1471. Fore Street.

ENTERTAINMENT

◆ Cinemas - Bartholomew Street West. Sidwell Street.

◆ Concerts- St Georges Hall, Market Street.

◆ Theatres- Barnfield Theatre, Barnfield Road. Exeter & Devon Arts Centre, Bradninch Place, Gandy Street. Northcott Theatre, University of Exeter Campus, Stocker Road, St David's (N of Exeter).

SPORT & LEISURE

◆ Parks & Gardens- Bull Meadow, Bull Meadow Road. Bury Meadow, North Road. Mount Radford Lawn, Topsham Road. Northernhay Gardens, Queen Street. Rougemont Gardens, Castle Street.

◆ Sports Centres - Clifton Hill Sports Centre, Clifton Hill (NE Exeter). County Ground Stadium, off Cowick Street. Exeter Arena Athletic Stadium, Summer Lane (NE Exeter). Pyramids Swimming & Leisure Centre, Heavitree Road Riverside Leisure Centre, The Plaza, Cowick Street. St James' Sports Centre, St James' High School, Summer Lane (NE Exeter). St Peter's Sports Centre, St Peter's High School, Quarry Lane (E Exeter). Wonford Sports Centre, Burnthouse Lane (SE Exeter).

◆ Ski Slope - Clifton Hill Sports Centre (as above).

◆ Swimming Pools - Northbrook Swimming Pool, Beacon Lane (NE Exeter). Pyramids Swimming & Leisure Centre (as above). Riverside Leisure Centre (as above).

◆ Ten Pin Bowling- Exeter Megabowl, Haven Banks Retail Park, Water Lane.

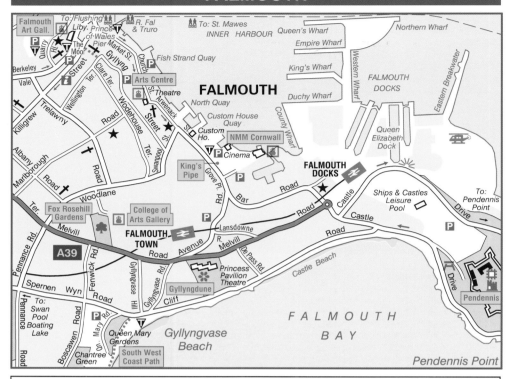

Falmouth Harbour and Carrick Roads form the largest natural haven in Britain. The port, developed in the 16th century by the Killigrew family, thrived by becoming a packet station for the Post Office between 1688 and 1852. It is now a major sailing centre with ship repair facilities centred on Falmouth Docks, best viewed from Castle Drive. Ferries to St Mawes, Flushing and along the River Fal to Truro leave from the Prince of Wales Pier. The town is noted for its gardens and parks with sub-tropical plants.

PLACES OF INTEREST

Tourist Information Centre (All year)- 28 Killigrew Street. Tel: 01326 312300

◆ FALMOUTH ART GALLERY - Changing art exhibitions in late 19th century Passmore Edwards Library. Municipal Buildings, The Moor.

◆ FALMOUTH ARTS CENTRE - Changing fine art exhibitions in four galleries. Paintings, sculpture, ceramics, photography & craft by local & national artists. 24 Church Street.

◆ FALMOUTH COLLEGE OF ARTS GALLERY - Students & visiting artists exhibitions. Falmouth College of Arts, Woodlane.

◆ FOX ROSEHILL GARDENS - 2 acre gardens containing exotic tree species including lemon, banana, eucalyptus & palms. Melvill Road.

◆ GYLLYNGDUNE GARDENS - Falmouth's finest formal gardens linked to seafront by a grotto walkway. Melvill Road.

◆ KING'S PIPE - Brick chimney once used to burn contraband tobacco. Arwenack Street.

◆ NATIONAL MARITIME MUSEUM CORNWALL - Purpose built £21.5 million outstation of the National Maritime Museum (Greenwich). Over 40 vessels. Boat, Cornwall & Environment Galleries. Viewing tower. Interactive displays. Discovery Quay.

◆ PENDENNIS CASTLE (EH) - Henry VIII castle with three storey circular keep & extensive outworks. Discovery Centre (Tudor gun-deck), WWII underground tunnels. Castle Drive.

ENTERTAINMENT

◆ Cinemas - Arwenack Street. Falmouth Arts Centre (see above).

◆ Theatres - Falmouth Arts Centre (see above). Princess Pavilion Theatre, Melvill Road.

SPORT & LEISURE

◆ Parks & Gardens - Fox Rosehill Gardens (see above). Gyllyngdune Gardens (see above). Kimberley Park, Kimberley Park Road (W Falmouth). Queen Mary Gardens, Queen Mary Road. Swan Pool Boating Lake, Swanpool Road (SW Falmouth).
Swimming Pools - Ships & Castles Leisure Pool, Castle Drive.

Fowey, one of the most important ports of medieval England, is situated on a deep water estuary used by bulk carriers for the export of china clay from the docks upstream. Justly famous for its beautiful harbour, with colourful yachts viewable from the Town Quay, the town has associations with novelist Daphne du Maurier who lived at Ferryside in Bodinnick and scholar and novelist Sir Arthur Quiller-Couch (known by the pseudonym 'Q') who lived at The Haven, Esplanade. The 15th century castellated mansion of Place is the home of the Treffry Family.

PLACES OF INTEREST

Tourist Information Centre (All year) - The Ticket Shop, 4 Custom House Hill. Tel: 01726 833616

◆ DAPHNE DU MAURIER LITERARY CENTRE - Exhibition & audio-visual display reflecting the novelists life & works. 5 South Street.

◆ FOWEY AQUARIUM - Marine aquarium exhibiting species caught locally. Old Town Hall, Town Quay.

◆ FOWEY MUSEUM - History of port of Fowey, ship models, local interest. Old Town Hall, Town Quay.

◆ HALL WALK (NT) - 16th century walk from Bodinnick to Penleath Point, where King Charles I was fired upon in 1644. (see 'Q' Memorial' below) ◆ HEADLAND GARDEN - 1 1/4 ac. cliff garden. Plants & trees resistant to salt-laden gales. Sub-tropical plants. 3 Battery Lane, Polruan. ◆ OLD HOUSE OF FOYE - Reputed oldest house in Fowey, c1430. Old kitchen, beams etc. Fore Street. ◆ POLRUAN & FOWEY BLOCKHOUSES - Built in the late 15th century either side of the harbour, a chain boom was hung between the blockhouses to prevent the entry of enemy vessels. Polruan Blockhouse is best preserved. ◆ ST CATHERINE'S CASTLE (EH) - Small defensive Henry VIII coastal fort c1530. Above Readymoney Cove. ◆ SIR ARTHUR QUILLER-COUCH MEMORIAL (NT) - Monument & famous viewpoint over Fowey, estuary & Pont Pill creek. Hall Walk, Bodinnick.

SPORT & LEISURE

◆ Parks & Gardens - Squires Field, Park Road.

Fowey

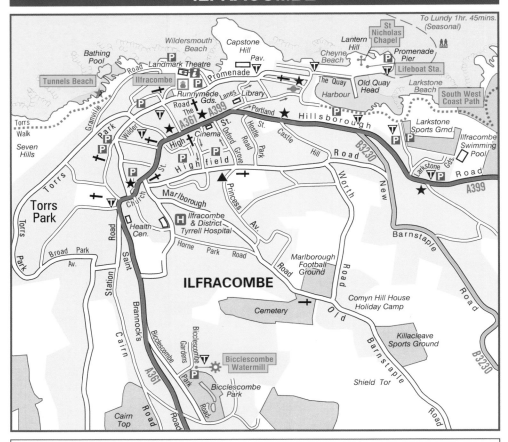

Ilfracombe, the picturesque town with its spectacular scenery and ancient harbour is North Devon's most popular seaside resort. The network of passages running from the High Street to the Sea Front known as 'The Lanes' enable the pedestrian to explore Ilfracombe along some of its oldest paths. A section has been developed into a sculpture trail with mosaics depicting various features characteristic of the town. The South West coastal path runs through Ilfracombe and the famous Torrs Walk heads out west to the village of Lee offering extensive views as you walk along the cliff top. In the summer months, the MS Oldenburg runs regular sailings to Lundy Island.

PLACES OF INTEREST
Tourist Information Centre (All year) - The Landmark Theatre, The Seafront. Tel: 01271 863001
◆ BICCLESCOMBE WATERMILL - Restored 18th century mill. Runs during the Summer for demonstration purposes only. Bicclescombe Park, Bicclescombe Gardens. ◆ ILFRACOMBE MUSEUM - Located in a building dating from 1885, this intriguing collection contains over 20,000 exhibits of natural history along with war memorabilia, paintings, photographs & Victoriana which reflect life of a bygone age. There is also a brass-rubbing centre. Runnymede Gardens, Wilder Road. ◆ LIFEBOAT STATION - Established 1828. Inflatable 'D' & Mersey Class lifeboats. Cove car park, The Quay. ◆ ST NICHOLAS CHAPEL - 14th century chapel has been used as a lighthouse to guide seafarers into the harbour since 1522. Small exhibition illustrating the history of the chapel & local area. Lantern Hill, The Quay.
◆ TUNNELS BEACH - Approximately 150 years ago, 4 tunnels were created by cutting through solid rock to provide access to this famous beach location. Granville Road.

ENTERTAINMENT
◆ Cinemas - 134 High Street. Landmark Theatre, The Promenade.
◆ Theatres - Landmark Theatre (see above).

SPORT & LEISURE
◆ Parks & Gardens - Bicclescombe Park, Bicclescombe Road. Runnymede Gardens, Wilder Road.
◆ Swimming Pools - Ilfracombe Swimming Pool, Hillsborough Road.

LAUNCESTON

Launceston, an ancient medieval hill top town, was the only walled town in Cornwall and until 1835 was the county's capital. Dunheved, the old town, is dominated by the castle and has many narrow twisting streets, of note being Castle Street with its brick Georgian houses. The town once had two railway stations at Newport served by two competing companies.

PLACES OF INTEREST

Tourist Information Centre (All year) - Market House Arcade, Market Street.
Tel: 01566 772321 / 772333

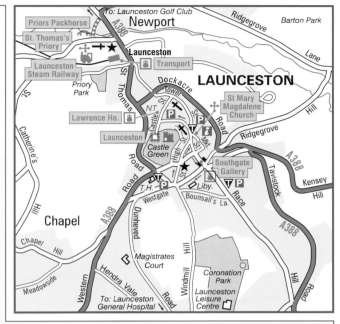

◆ LAUNCESTON CASTLE (EH) - Norman motte with shell keep & cylindrical tower providing commanding views. Castle Street. ◆ LAUNCESTON STEAM RAILWAY - 2 mile 2ft. gauge steam railway using Victorian locomotives on route of former North Cornwall line. Stations at Launceston, Hunts Crossing, Deer Park & Newmills (picnic site). Launceston Station, Newport Industrial Estate, St Thomas Road. ◆ LAUNCESTON STEAM RAILWAY TRANSPORT MUSEUM - Vintage cars, motorcycles, stationary steam engines. Launceston Steam Railway (see above).
◆ LAWRENCE HOUSE MUSEUM (NT) - Georgian house of 1753 housing museum of local history. Victorian dressing room & costumes. 9 Castle Street. ◆ PRIORS PACKHORSE BRIDGE - Ancient five arched packhorse bridge over River Kensey. Westbridge Road. ◆ ST MARY MAGDALENE CHURCH - Exterior adorned with decorative carvings (apart from tower) datings from early 16th century. Church Street.
◆ ST THOMAS'S PRIORY - Ruins of 12th century Augustinian Priory behind St Thomas's church. Riverside. ◆ SOUTHGATE GALLERY - Art gallery in room above the narrow arch of Southgate, a surviving part of the former 16th century town walls. Southgate Street.

SPORT & LEISURE

◆ Parks & Gardens - Castle Green, Castle Street. Coronation Park, Dunheved Road.
◆ Sports Centres - Launceston Leisure Centre, Coronation Park, Dunheved Road.
◆ Swimming Pools - Launceston Leisure Centre (as above)

Ilfracombe

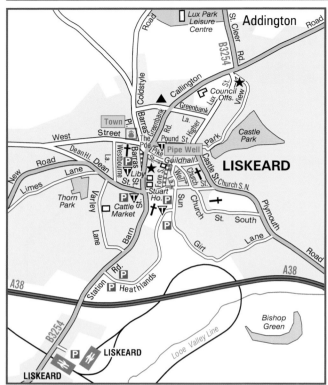

Liskeard, one of four former Stannary (or coinage) towns for the tin industry, is a busy hill top market town. The town has many fine Georgian buildings in the Parade, the 1850s Italian style Victorian Guildhall with tall clock tower in Pike Street and the late 19th century Passmore Edwards Library, together with Stuart House, in Barras Street. Castle Park is the former site of the castle and at 150 m (492 ft) provides good views. The Looe Valley Line is a scenic 8.5 mile branch railway line to Looe.

PLACES OF INTEREST
◆ LISKEARD TOWN MUSEUM- Local history of Liskeard. 5 West Street. ◆ PIPE WELL - Four spout well never known to dry up, also known as St Martins Well, on site of Market Hall. Well Lane.

SPORT & LEISURE
◆ Parks & Gardens - Castle Park, Castle Street. Thorn Park, Limes Lane. ◆ Sports Centres - Lux Park Leisure Centre, Coldstyle Road. ◆ Swimming Pools - Lux Park Leisure Centre (as above).

Looe is a busy fishing port famous as a shark fishing centre. Situated on a narrow estuary at the confluence of the two Looe rivers it is divided into East Looe with its small narrow streets and West Looe, its quieter counterpart, linked together by a bridge built in 1855. A fish market is held on Buller Quay and the beach near the Banjo Pier is popular. The Looe Valley Line is a scenic 8.5 mile branch railway line to Liskeard.

PLACES OF INTEREST
Tourist Information Centre (Summer only) - The Guildhall, Fore Street, East Looe. Tel: 01503 262072
◆ LIFEBOAT STATION - Established in 1992. Inflatable 'D' lifeboat. Buller Quay, Buller Street, East Looe. ◆ LIVING FROM THE SEA AQUARIUM - Species caught around the Cornish coast. World of Sharks Exhibition. History of the Cornish fisherman. Buller Quay, East Looe. ◆ OLD GUILDHALL MUSEUM - 15th century guildhall. Displays on local history, fishing, boat building & smuggling. Exhibits include toys, model ships & the old cells. Higher Market Street, East Looe. ◆ SOUTH EAST CORNWALL DISCOVERY CENTRE - Visitor centre with displays on wildlife & heritage of SE Cornwall. Video & photographic exhibition. Millpool, West Looe.

ENTERTAINMENT
◆ Cinemas - Higher Market Street, East Looe.

SPORT & LEISURE
◆ Parks & Gardens - Hannafore Road, West Looe. West Looe Downs, West Road, West Looe.

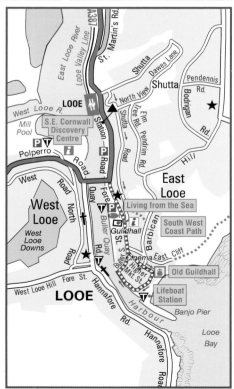

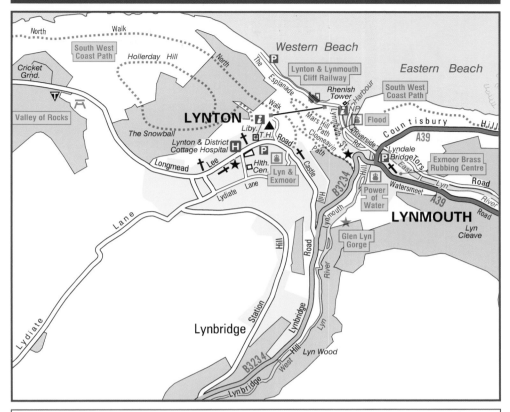

Separated vertically by 152 m (500 ft), the twin villages of Lynton and Lynmouth are linked by a unique water powered cliff railway. The vulnerability of Lynmouth's location lying on the shore where the valleys of the East and West Lyn converge made it the victim of the 1952 flood when 90 million gallons of water fell in a single night. The Rhenish Tower which was originally built in 1855 by Colonel Rawdon was rebuilt following its destruction in the disaster. Lynmouth was once famous for its large catches of herring and curing houses known as 'Red Herring Houses' lined both sides of the river. Lynton and Lynmouth developed rapidly as a tourist destination with its natural beauty and tranquility making it a favourable destination for the traveller. Today numerous walks exemplify the natural beauty of the area; paths over Hollerday Hill lead to the Valley of Rocks and Mars Hill is renowned for its thatched cottages.

PLACES OF INTEREST

Tourist Information Centre (All year) - Town Hall, Lee Road, Lynton. Tel: 01598 752225

◆ EXMOOR BRASS RUBBING CENTRE - Houses over 100 brass facsimiles dating from 1277. The collection which includes knights, clergy & animals is one of the largest available to the public. Woodside Craft Centre, Watersmeet Road, Lynmouth.

◆ GLEN LYN GORGE - Walks lead up through the woodland passing cascades & waterfalls to the ravine. Flood level marks from the 1952 catastrophe can be seen & England's largest privately owned hydro-electric station opened here in 1985. Watersmeet Road, Lynmouth.

◆ LYN & EXMOOR MUSEUM - Housed in a 17th century cottage the museum offers a comprehensive reflection of life in the area from the stone age to the modern day. St Vincent Cottage, Market Street, Lynton. ◆ LYNMOUTH FLOOD EXHIBITION - Exhibition recalls the devastation caused by the flood of 1952. Memorial Hall, Riverside Road, Lynmouth. ◆ LYNMOUTH VISITOR CENTRE (NP) - Displays recall the famous rescue of 1899 when the Lynmouth lifeboat was hauled 13 miles over land to launch at Porlock Weir. The Esplanade, Lynmouth. ◆ LYNTON & LYNMOUTH CLIFF RAILWAY - Officially opened in 1890, the railway is the last working water powered Victorian cliff railway in Europe. Rises 152 m (500 ft) over the 263 m (862 ft) of track from Lynmouth to Lynton. The Esplanade, Lynmouth & Lee Road, Lynton.

◆ POWER OF WATER EXHIBITION - Displays illustrate the various uses of water. Exhibition of steam engine models. Old Chapel, Glen Lyn Gorge, Watersmeet Road, Lynmouth.

◆ VALLEY OF ROCKS, THE - Famous dry valley thought to be a glacial meltwater channel formed during the Ice Age. Other formations include Castle Rock, Ragged Jack & Devil's Cheesewring. Lynton.

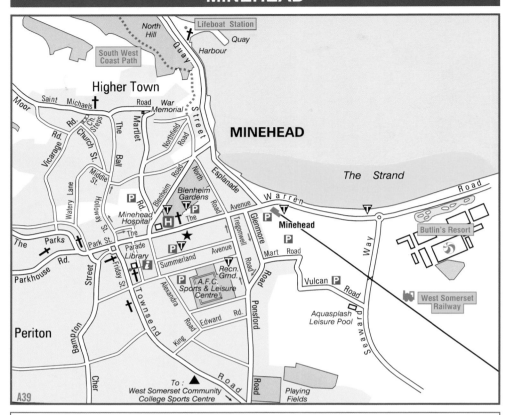

The popular holiday resort of Minehead lies on the north eastern edge of Exmoor between the National Park and the coast. The development of the town centred around the quay which offered safety and shelter on a coastal front that was both exposed and hazardous. The Higher Town retains much of its charm with thatched cottages and narrow alleyways, a favourite is Church Steps which leads up to the 14th century St Michael's Church on North Hill with spectacular views over the town. The old almhouses are on Market House Lane and nearby are the picturesque Blenheim Gardens. Minehead is the starting point of Britain's longest footpath, the 500 mile South West Coast Path.

PLACES OF INTEREST

Tourist Information Centre (All year) - 17 Friday Street. Tel: 01643 702624

◆ BUTLIN'S FAMILY ENTERTAINMENT RESORT - Large entertainment complex offering a diverse range of activities including sub-tropical waterworld with flume rides & rapids, funfair, leisure dome & boating lake. The Seafront, Warren Road.

◆ LIFEBOAT STATION - Established in 1901. Atlantic 75 class & Inflatable 'D' lifeboats. The Harbour.

◆ WEST SOMERSET RAILWAY - Steam trains run from Minehead to Bishop's Lydeard on the line that was closed by British Rail in 1971. The reopening of the line in 1976 created the longest independent railway in Britain. The Station, The Sea Front.

ENTERTAINMENT

◆ Cinemas - Butlin's Family Entertainment Resort (see above).
◆ Theatre - Regal Theatre, The Avenue.

SPORT & LEISURE

◆ Parks & Gardens - Blenheim Gardens, Blenheim Road.
◆ Sports Centres - West Somerset Community College Sports Centre, Bircham Road (SE Minehead).
◆ Swimming Pools - Aquasplash Leisure Pool, Seaward Way. Butlin's Somerwest World Holiday Centre (see above).
◆ Ten Pin Bowling - Butlin's Family Entertainment Resort (see above).

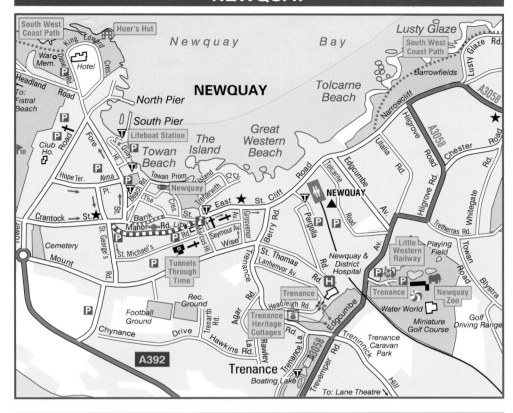

Newquay, Cornwall's favourite holiday resort, is famous for its Atlantic rollers, making it a centre for surfing, and for its expanses of sandy beaches of which west facing Fistral Beach (to the west of the town) is the largest and most popular. Once important as a fishing port, due largely to huge shoals of pilchards, and for the export of china clay, the town became a tourist destination with the coming of the railway in 1875.

PLACES OF INTEREST
Tourist Information Centre (All year) - Municipal Offices, Marcus Hill. Tel: 01637 871345
◆ HUER'S HUT - Small clifftop building from which the Huer watched for pilchard shoals. King Edward Crescent. ◆ LIFEBOAT STATION - Established in 1860. Atlantic 75 & Inflatable 'D' lifeboats. South Quay, Newquay Harbour. ◆ LITTLE WESTERN RAILWAY - 7.25" gauge circular miniature railway. Trenance Leisure Park, Edgcumbe Avenue. ◆ NEWQUAY SEA LIFE AQUARIUM - 70 species. Sharks, stingrays, seahorses. Lair of the Octopus. Underwater tunnel. Towan Promenade. ◆ NEWQUAY ZOO - 10 acres of lakeside gardens with over 300 animals. Tropical & Nocturnal Houses, Animal encounters, Dragon Maze. Trenance Leisure Park, Edgcumbe Avenue. ◆ TRENANCE HERITAGE COTTAGES - Displays of Cornish way of life in the 1900's. Trenance Gardens, Trenance Road.
◆ TRENANCE GARDENS - Outstanding municipal gardens, boating lake. Trenance Road.
◆ TRENANCE LEISURE PARK - 26 acre sport & leisure park. Edgcumbe Avenue.
◆ TUNNELS THROUGH TIME - Recreation of the stories & legends of Cornwall using life-size figures. St Michaels Road.

ENTERTAINMENT
◆ Theatres - Lane Theatre, Lane (SE of Newquay).

SPORT & LEISURE
◆ Parks & Gardens - Trenance Gardens (see above). Trenance Leisure Park (see above).
◆ Sports Centres - Newquay Sports Centre, Tretherras Road (E Newquay).
◆ Swimming Pools - Newquay Water World, Trenance Leisure Park.

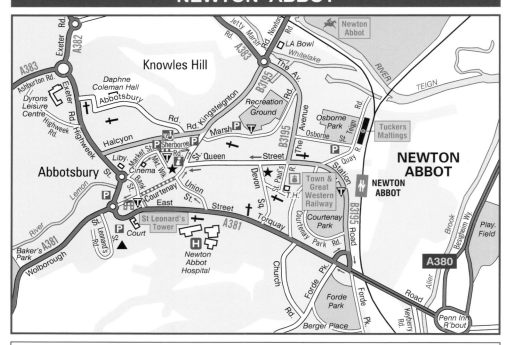

Newton Abbot is a busy market town and, since the arrival of the South Devon Railway in the mid 19th century, a railway town with typical railway terraces. It is situated at the head of the River Teign estuary where the Stover Canal brought down clay, and granite from quarries on Dartmoor served by the Haytor Granite Tramway, for export. The Templer Way follows much of the route.

PLACES OF INTEREST
Tourist Information Centre (All year) - 6 Bridge House, Courtenay Street. Tel: 01626 367494
◆ NEWTON ABBOT RACECOURSE - Between Newton Abbot & Kingsteignton. Newton Road.
◆ NEWTON ABBOT TOWN & GREAT WESTERN RAILWAY MUSEUM - History of town & its railway. Working signal box. GWR artifacts & photographs. 2a St Paul's Road.
◆ ST LEONARD'S TOWER - 14th century clock-tower (the remains of St Leonard's Church) where William III, Prince of Orange, was declared king in 1688. Courtenay Street.
◆ TUCKERS MALTINGS - Guided tours of traditional working malthouse where barley is turned into malt using original Victorian machinery. Teign Road, Osborne Park.

ENTERTAINMENT
◆ Cinemas - Market Street.

SPORT & LEISURE
◆ Parks & Gardens - Baker's Park, Wolborough Street. Courtenay Park, Courtenay Park Road. Forde Park, Forde Park. Osborne Park, Osborne Street.
◆ Sports Centres - Dyrons Leisure Centre, Wain Lane.
◆ Swimming Pools - Dyrons Leisure Centre (as above).
◆ Ten-Pin Bowling - LA Bowl, Kingsteignton Road.

Fore Street, Totnes

Padstow is a popular resort on the River Camel Estuary. A fishing port with narrow winding streets converging on the picturesque and ancient harbour, the town was once the western outpost of the London & South Western Railway, closed in 1967 and now the Camel Trail. The pagan 'Obby 'Oss festival is held on May Day to celebrate the coming of Summer. There are no beaches in Padstow however a ferry leaves from the North Quay, or Lower Beach at low tide, to beaches at Rock across the estuary.

PLACES OF INTEREST

Tourist Information Centre (All year) - Red Brick Building, North Quay. Tel: 01841 533449

◆ CAMEL TRAIL - Popular 17 mile cycleway & footpath on former railway line starting at Padstow and linking to Wadebridge & Bodmin.

◆ PADSTOW MUSEUM - Local history. Displays on Padstow lifeboat, customs, railway. Ship paintings. Town Library, The Institute, Market Place.

◆ PRIDEAUX PLACE - Elizabethan mansion completed in 1592. Formal garden & landscaped deer park. Tregirls Lane.

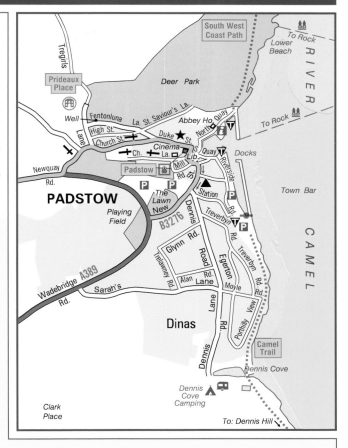

ENTERTAINMENT
◆ Cinemas- Lanadwell Street.

SPORT & LEISURE
◆ Parks & Gardens- The Lawn, New Street.

Padstow Harbour

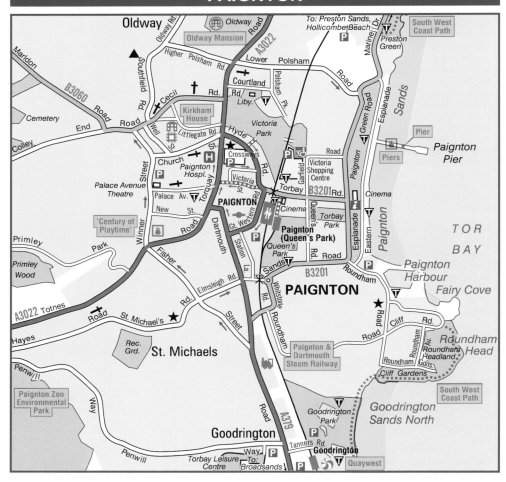

Paignton is a very popular family seaside resort which developed as a close neighbour of Torquay after the arrival of the railway in the mid 19th century. There are gardens, a pier, a long seafront (with the sandy beach of Paignton Sands adjacent to Paignton Green) and a small harbour at the end of the Esplanade. Other popular sandy beaches are Goodrington Sands, Broadsands to the south, and Preston Sands and Hollicombe Beach.

PLACES OF INTEREST
Tourist Information Centre (All year) - multiplex cinema, The Esplanade. Tel: 01803 558383
◆ 'CENTURY OF PLAYTIME'- DOLL & TOY MUSEUM - Old dolls & toys. 30 Winner Street.
◆ KIRKHAM HOUSE (EH) - 15th century stone merchant's town house. Old hall, furniture displays. Kirkham Street. ◆ OLDWAY MANSION - Begun by Isaac Singer (founder of the famous sewing machine company) in 1875 in the style of the Palace of Versailles with 17 acres of landscaped gardens. Torquay Road.
◆ PAIGNTON & DARTMOUTH STEAM RAILWAY - 7 mile standard gauge steam railway running along the scenic Torbay coast & Dart estuary to Kingswear. Stations also at Goodrington & Churston. Paignton (Queen's Park) Station, Torbay Road. ◆ PAIGNTON PIER & PIERS MUSEUM - Amusements, childrens rides, old slot machines. Paignton Sands. ◆ PAIGNTON ZOO ENVIROMENTAL PARK - 75 acres of gardens with lions, tigers, elephant & giraffe house, ape centre, baboon rock, aviary.- Totnes Road. ◆ QUAYWEST - Waterpark with 8 water flumes including the highest in England at 20 m (65 ft). Swimming pools, amusement rides. Goodrington Sands.

ENTERTAINMENT
◆ Cinemas - Esplanade Road. Torbay Road. Theatres- Palace Avenue Theatre, Palace Avenue.
SPORT & LEISURE
◆ Parks & Gardens - Goodrington Park, Tanners Rd. Oldway, Torquay Rd.Paignton Green, Eastern Esplanade. Preston Green, Marine Drive. Queen's Park, Queen's Road. Roundham Headland & Cliff Gardens, Roundham Gardens. Torbay Park, Esplanade Road. Victoria Park, Hyde Road. ◆ Sports Centres - Torbay Leisure Centre, Clennon Valley, Penwill Way. ◆ Swimming Pools - Quaywest (see above). Torbay Leisure Centre (as above).

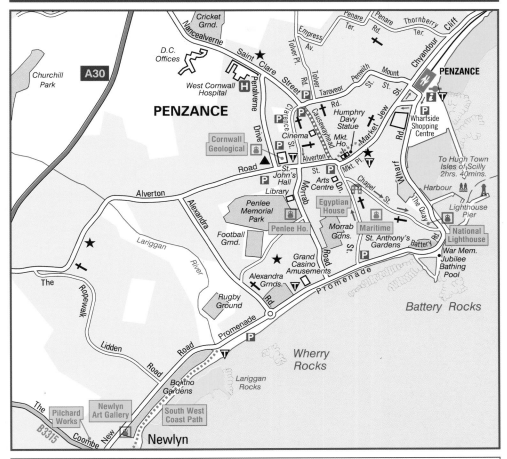

Penzance, a port and resort characterized by its 19th century granite buildings, has developed as a market town for West Cornwall, its status being promoted by becoming the western terminus of the former Great Western Railway. Buildings of note include the imposing domed Market House (1838) at the top of Market Jew Street with the statue of Sir Humphry Davy (born 1778), inventor of the miner's safety lamp, below it and St John's Hall on Alverton Street, built in the 1860s, one of the largest granite buildings in Britain. There are two parks with sub-tropical plants off Morrab Road. Regular ferries leave Lighthouse Pier for St Mary's in the Isles of Scilly; helicopter flights leave from the heliport off the A30 to the east of the town.

PLACES OF INTEREST
Tourist Information Centre (All year) - Station Road. Tel: 01736 362207
◆ CORNWALL GEOLOGICAL MUSEUM - Cornish rocks, minerals & fossils. Mining & quarrying displays. St John's Hall, Alverton Street. ◆ EGYPTIAN HOUSE - Building with elaborate painted Eygptian style facade built in 1836. Chapel Street. ◆ NEWLYN ART GALLERY- Changing exhibitions of contemporary paintings & sculpture in Passmore Edwards building. Newlyn Green, New Road, Newlyn. ◆ PENLEE HOUSE GALLERY & MUSEUM - History of West Cornwall from stone age to present day. Largest art collection in West Cornwall dating from 1750 including artists of the famous Newlyn School. Morrab Road. ◆ PENZANCE MARITIME MUSEUM - Full size recreation of part of early 18th century warship. Treasure & artefacts recovered by diving expeditions. 19 Chapel Street. ◆ PILCHARD WORKS - Britain's last working salt pilchard factory. Factory visit to press room & heritage centre with photographs, paintings & artefacts. Tolcarne, The Coombe, Newlyn. ◆ TRINITY HOUSE NATIONAL LIGHTHOUSE CENTRE - Story of lighthouses. Lighthouse equipment, model ships, buoys, reconstructed lighthouse room. Old Buoy Store, Wharf Road.

ENTERTAINMENT
◆ Cinemas - Causewayhead. Theatres - West Cornwall Arts Centre, Parade Street.
SPORT & LEISURE
◆ Parks & Gardens - Alexandra Grounds, Promenade. Bolitho Gardens, New Road, Newlyn. Morrab Gardens, Morrab Road. Penlee Memorial Park, Morrab Road. St Anthony's Gardens, Battery Road. ◆ Swimming Pools - Jubilee Bathing Pool, Battery Road. ◆ Ten-Pin Bowling - Grand Casino Amusements, Promenade.

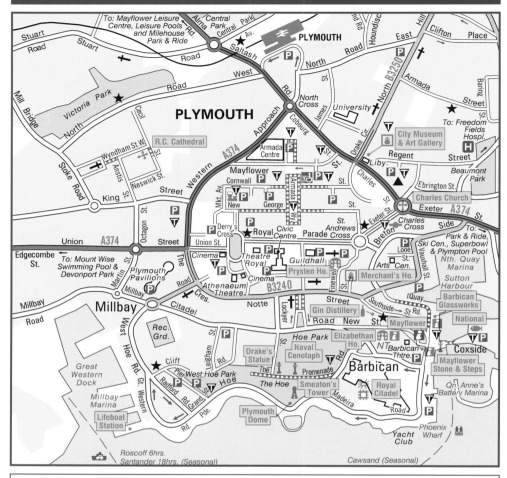

Plymouth is the largest city in the West Country. Associated with sailors such as Hawkins, Raleigh, Frobisher and Sir Francis Drake, the harbour of Plymouth Sound (protected by Rennie's one mile long breakwater of 1812-41), is a safe anchorage leading to the 300 acre Royal Navy Dockyard of Devonport founded in 1691. Pleasure cruises to view the warships depart from the Mayflower Steps and Phoenix Wharf. Much of the city centre (now rebuilt) was destroyed during a bombing raid in 1941, however, the Barbican area, part of the old quarter of Plymouth with narrow streets, survives.

Plymouth Barbican

Drakes Island, Plymouth

PLACES OF INTEREST

Tourist Information Centre (All year) - Island House, The Barbican. Tel: 01752 304849

◆ BARBICAN GLASSWORKS - Glassmaking demonstrations. Visitor centre with information on the maritime & trading history of the Barbican & Sutton Harbour. Old Fishmarket, The Barbican.

◆ CITY MUSEUM & ART GALLERY - Collections of West Country art & porcelain including works by Sir Joshua Reynolds. Natural history. Drake Circus.

◆ CHARLES CHURCH - Bombed building & spire of 17th century church, left as a memorial to Plymouth's war dead. Charles Cross.

◆ DRAKE'S STATUE - Statue of 1884 of Sir Francis Drake overlooking The Hoe, where according to legend he was playing bowls when the Spanish Armada was first sighted in 1588. The Promenade, The Hoe.

◆ ELIZABETHAN HOUSE (NT) - Tudor sea captain's timber framed house. Period furnishings. National Trust Information centre. 32 New Street.

◆ LIFEBOAT STATION - Established in 1803. Arun lifeboat. Millbay Marina, Great Western Road.

◆ MAYFLOWER STONE & STEPS - Memorial stone & steps where the Pilgrim Fathers sailed to America in 1620. The Barbican.

◆ MAYFLOWER VISITOR CENTRE - Story of the Pilgrim Fathers. The Barbican.

◆ MERCHANT'S HOUSE MUSEUM - 16th century Elizabethan building housing displays on the story of Plymouth including the Eddystone lighthouses, Plymouth's defences & the blitz. Victorian pharmacy. 33 St Andrews Street.

◆ NATIONAL MARINE AQUARIUM - UK's biggest aquarium with deepest tank in the UK. Deep Reef tank, Coral Seas tanks, Shark Theatre, World of Seahorses, Mediterranean tank, The Abyss. Plymouth Sound sealife, seashore life & rare preserved Giant Squid. Rope Walk, Coxside.

◆ NAVAL CENOTAPH - Tall monument commemorating those who died in both world wars. The Promenade, The Hoe.

◆ PLYMOUTH DOME - Life size replica Elizabethan Street. Displays include Plymouth seafarers, blitz devastation & ocean liners. Observation galleries over Plymouth Sound. The Hoe.

◆ PLYMOUTH GIN DISTILLERY - Guided Tours of 200 year old distillery on site of former friary. Audio-visual. Black Friars Distillery, 60 Southside Street.

◆ PLYMOUTH ROMAN CATHOLIC CATHEDRAL - Gothic Revival building of 1858 with 61 m (200 ft) spire. Cecil Street.

◆ PRYSTEN HOUSE - Stone built merchant's town house of 1498. Finewell Street.

◆ ROYAL CITADEL (EH) - Guided tours of England's largest 17th century fortress including Baroque main gate & royal chapel. The Hoe.

Smeaton's Tower, The Hoe Plymouth

◆ SMEATON'S TOWER - Upper part of third Eddystone lighthouse built by John Smeaton in 1759, removed to The Hoe in 1882 when the sea undermined the rock on which it stood. The Hoe.

ENTERTAINMENT

◆ Cinemas - Derry's Cross (two). Plymouth Arts Centre, Looe Street. ◆ Concerts - Plymouth Pavilions, Millbay Road. ◆ Theatres - Athenaeum Theatre, Derry's Cross. Barbican Theatre, Castle St. Theatre Royal, Royal Parade.

SPORT & LEISURE

◆ Ice Rink - Swiss Lake Ice Rink, Plymouth Pavilions, Millbay Road. ◆ Parks & Gardens - Beaumont Park, Tothill Avenue. Central Park, Alma Road. Devonport Park, Exmouth Road, Devonport (W Plymouth) Freedom Fields, Lipson Road (E Plymouth). Hoe Park, West Hoe Park & The Hoe. Victoria Park, North Road West. ◆ Ski Slope - Plymouth Ski Centre, Longbridge Road (NE Plymouth). ◆ Sports Centres - Mayflower Leisure Centre, Central Park, Mayflower Drive. ◆ Swimming Pools - Atlantis Pool, Plymouth Pavilions, Millbay Road. Central Park Leisure Pools, Central Park, Mayflower Drive. Mount Wise Swimming Pool, Richmond Walk, Mount Wise (W Plymouth). Plympton Pool, Harewood Park, Plympton (NE of Plymouth). Seaton Pool, Brest Road, Crownhill (N Plymouth). ◆ Ten-Pin Bowling - Plymouth Superbowl, Plymouth Road, Plympton (NE of Plymouth).

St. Ives, formerly one of the most important pilchard fisheries in Cornwall, is now a very popular holiday resort of great charm characterized by the old fishing quarter with its narrow steep cobbled streets, alleys and steps lined with stone cottages. Its setting and clarity of light led to its colonization by artists, notably Ben Nicholson and Barbara Hepworth in 1939. Beyond the harbour, with Smeaton's Pier, is The Island, a headland separating sheltered Porthgwidden Beach from Porthmeor Beach popular for surfing.

PLACES OF INTEREST

Tourist Information Centre (All year) - The Guildhall, Street-an-Pol.
Tel: 01736 796297

◆ BARBARA HEPWORTH MUSEUM & SCULPTURE GARDEN- The artists former workshop displaying over 40 of her sculptures. Trewyn Studios, Barnoon Hill.

◆ LIFEBOAT STATION- Established in 1840. Mersey & Inflatable 'D' lifeboats. West Pier, St. Ives Harbour.

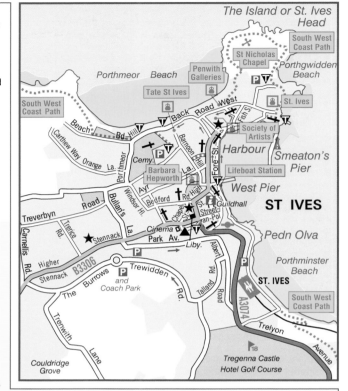

◆ PENWITH GALLERIES- Exhibitions of paintings & sculpture by the Penwith Society of Arts. Back Road West. ◆ ST IVES MUSEUM- Cornish & local history. Displays on fishing, lifeboat, maritime history, railways. Wheal Dream. St. Ives Society of Artists- Paintings & sculptures. Old Mariner's Church, Norway Square. ◆ ST NICHOLAS CHAPEL- Fishermans chapel which exhibited a guiding light prior to the lighthouses on Smeaton's Pier. The Island. ◆ TATE ST IVES - Outpost of London's Tate Gallery. Changing displays of 20th century modern art associated with St. Ives & Cornwall. Porthmeor Beach.

ENTERTAINMENT
◆ Cinemas - Royal Square.

SPORT & LEISURE
◆ Parks & Gardens - Trewyn Gardens, Back Street.

St. Ives

TAUNTON

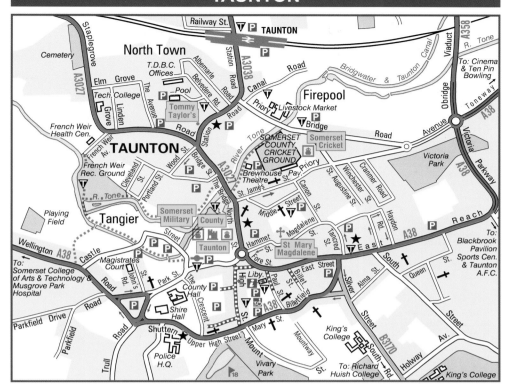

Founded in the 7th century by King Ina to guard the river crossing against the Celts, Taunton, 'the town on the Tone' is the county town of Somerset and home of the county's cricket ground. History has left its mark on the town and the heritage trail highlights many of the towns architectural features using distinctive brass plaques set in the pavement. Buildings of interest include the 14th century Tudor House in Fore Street, the oldest house in Taunton and Gray's Almshouses founded in 1635 by Robert Gray. Taunton developed in the 13th century as an important market and trading town. Today with a population of 60,000, it is still a lively centre with a diverse range of shopping facilities and a livestock market.

PLACES OF INTEREST
Tourist Information Centre (All year) - The Library, Paul Street. Tel: 01823 336344
◆ ST MARY MAGDALENE CHURCH - One of the largest & richest perpendicular churches in England. The 49.7m (163ft) tower dating from 1500 was rebuilt in the 19th century & local legend tells of how donkeys were used in the construction to haul the ropes of the pulley system to raise materials to the top. Upon completion of the tower, the donkeys were themselves raised to the top so they could see the view. Magdalene Street. ◆ SOMERSET COUNTY MUSEUM - A wide variety of exhibits are combined to reflect the history of Somerset. The collection includes dolls, toys, silver, pottery, fossils & archaeological items. Taunton Castle, Castle Green. ◆ SOMERSET CRICKET MUSEUM - Housed in a renovated priory barn, this extensive collection of cricket memorabilia reflects the history of the County Club from 1875. Adjacent to the County Cricket Ground. Priory Barn, 7 Priory Avenue. ◆ SOMERSET MILITARY MUSEUM, THE - Exhibition devoted to the history of the Somerset Light Infantry. Somerset County Museum, Taunton Castle, Castle Green. ◆ TAUNTON CASTLE - The remains of the 12th century castle now form part of the County Museum in the town centre. The Great Hall which survives today with some modifications was the scene of Judge Jeffries notorious Bloody Assize held after the collapse of Monmouth's Rebellion in 1685. Castle Green. ◆ TOMMY TAYLOR'S - Action packed all weather attraction for children, includes rope bridges, climbing nets, ball pool & spiral slides. 43 Station Road.

ENTERTAINMENT
◆ Cinemas- Heron Gate (E Taunton). Theatres- Brewhouse Theatre & Arts Centre, Coal Orchard.
SPORT & LEISURE
◆ Parks & Gardens - French Weir Park, French Weir Avenue. Goodland Gardens, Castle Street. Victoria Park, Victoria Parkway. Vivary Park, Mount Street.
◆ Sports Centre - Blackbrook Pavilion Sports Centre, Blackbrook Way (SE Taunton).
◆ Swimming Pools - Taunton Pool, Station Road.
◆ Ten Pin Bowling - Hollywood Bowling, Heron Gate (E Taunton).

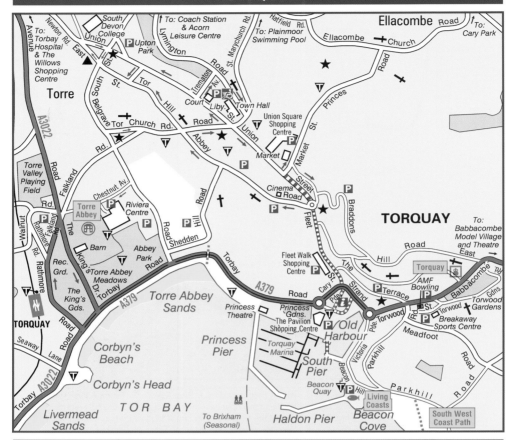

Tor Bay with the three main towns of Torquay, Paignton and Brixham is known as the 'English Riviera' due to the mild climate which supports gardens planted with sub-tropical plants including many palms, similar to those originally imported from New Zealand and the Mediterranean in the early 19th century. The planned streets of the town were first developed by the Cary family of Torre Abbey, the characteristic terraces being built in the first half of the 19th century. The harbour and Torquay Marina provide the focus for the town with the main shopping street of Union Street accessible via Fleet Walk. Torre Abbey Sands, one of over 20 beaches on the Riviera, provides a nearby sandy beach.

PLACES OF INTEREST
Tourist Information Centre (All year)- Vaughan Parade. Tel: 01803 297428
◆ LIVING COASTS - Largest aquarium in the West. Exotic tropical marine fish & local marine life. Reptiles & birds. Ground floor, multi-storey car park, Beacon Quay, Strand. ◆ TORQUAY MUSEUM - Local history, regimental, archaeology & natural history galleries. Victoriana. Agatha Christie exhibition. 529 Babbacombe Road. ◆ TORRE ABBEY - 18th century house with furnished period rooms, art galleries, chapel, formal gardens on remains of Premonstratensian abbey (founded in 1196) of which the gatehouse, guest hall & tithe (or Spanish) barn survive. The King's Drive.

ENTERTAINMENT
◆ Cinemas - Abbey Road. Theatres - Babbacombe Theatre, Babbacombe Downs, Babbacombe (N of Torquay). Princess Theatre, Torbay Road.

SPORT & LEISURE
◆ Parks & Gardens - Abbey Park (& Torre Abbey Meadows), Torbay Road. Cary Park, Cary Avenue, Babbacombe (N of Torquay). Princess Gardens, Torbay Road. Torwood Gardens, Torwood Gardens Road. Upton Park, Lymington Road. Victoria Park, Sherwell Lane (W Torquay). ◆ Sports Centres - Acorn Leisure Centre, Lichfield Avenue (N Torquay). Breakaway Sports Centre, Torwood Gardens Road. Riviera Centre, Chestnut Avenue. ◆ Swimming Pools - Riviera Centre (as above). Plainmoor Swimming Pool (Swim Torquay), Plainmoor (N of Torquay). ◆ Ten-Pin Bowling - AMF Bowling, Torwood Street.

TRURO

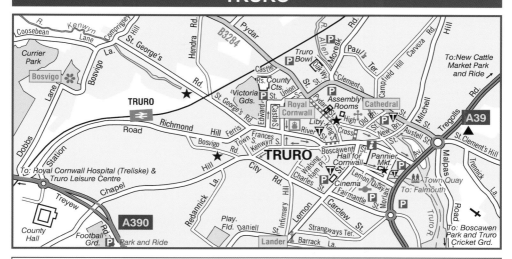

Truro grew up as a tin and copper exporting port on the navigable Truro River, and prospered from becoming a stannary town in the 18th century. Now Cornwall's cathedral city and administrative centre, the city is famous for its Georgian architecture exemplified by Boscawen Street, Strangways Terrace, Walsingham Place and Lemon Street (the finest Georgian Street in Cornwall). Buildings of note are the former Assembly Rooms of 1772 on High Cross and the granite City Hall built in the Italian style. Boat trips to Falmouth operate from Town Quay (or Malpas when the tide is low).

PLACES OF INTEREST

Tourist Information Centre (All year) - Municipal Buildings, City Hall, Boscawen Street. Tel: 01872 274555
◆ BOSVIGO GARDEN - 3 acres of enclosed & walled gardens with herbaceous & rare plants. Bosvigo Lane.
◆ LANDER MONUMENT - Tall granite column with statue of Richard Lander, killed exploring the River Niger in West Africa. Lemon Street.
◆ ROYAL CORNWALL MUSEUM - Displays include archaeology, local history, mining industry, seafaring, natural history, costumes, fine art. River Street.
◆ TRURO CATHEDRAL - Built between 1880 & 1910 in the Early English style; the first Anglican cathedral to be built in England since the rebuilding of St Paul's and the only cathedral in Cornwall. High Cross.

ENTERTAINMENT
◆ Cinemas - Lemon Street.
◆ Theatres - City Hall, Boscawen Street.

SPORT & LEISURE
◆ Parks & Gardens -
Boscawen Park, Malpas Road (SE of Truro).
Victoria Gardens, Castle Rise.
◆ Sports Centres -
Truro Leisure Centre, College Road (W of Truro).
◆ Swimming Pools -
Truro Leisure Centre (as above).
◆ Ten-Pin Bowling -
Truro Bowl, Oak Way.

Torbay Harbour

BODMIN MOOR

Bodmin Moor, designated an area of outstanding natural beauty, is a remote, bleak heather covered upland granite moorland still grazed by moorland ponies and bisected by the main A30 road. Similar, but smaller and lower than Dartmoor, it was densely populated in the bronze age and has many archaeological remains. The best known are the three stone circles of The Hurlers, Rillaton Barrow and the hill fort of Stowe's Pound all near Minions, and the Stripple Stones Henge and Trippet Stone Circle on Hawkstor Downs near Blisland.

Natural features include Brown Willy, at 420 m (1,377 ft), the highest point on both Bodmin Moor and in Cornwall, and the rockier Roughtor, the second highest point, readily accesible from Camelford with over seventy hut circles on its north west slope. The Cheesewring, at Stowe's Hill near Minions, is a popular wind eroded granite formation of circular stones balanced on top of each other whilst the natural lake of Dozmary Pool, in the centre of the moor south of Bolventor, is according to legend where Sir Bedivere threw King Arthur's Sword Excalibur. Also at Bolventor is Jamaica Inn featured in the novel of the same name by Daphne du Maurier with Smugglers at Jamaica Inn tableaux & Daphne du Maurier memorial room.

Ruins of tin and copper mines can be seen to the south east of the moor at Minions and include the ruined engine houses of the Phoenix United and South Phoenix Mines. The Minions Heritage Centre is in Houseman's Engine House. Other attractions include Golitha Falls, managed by English Nature at the southern edge of the moor near Redgate and Wesley Cottage at Trewint, near Altarnun, where John Wesley, the founder of Methodism, stayed. There are reservoirs at Colliford Lake and Siblyback Lake Water Park.

Bodmin Moor

DARTMOOR

Dartmoor, one of the last great wildernesses of southern England, is a 365 square mile bleak granite upland with an average elevation of 366 m (1200 ft), designated a National Park in 1951. It is characterized by its coarse granite outcrops, or tors, and by large areas of isolated blanket peat bog covered with purple gorse and heather which provide rough grazing for the semi-wild Dartmoor ponies. The rapidly changing weather conditions, frequently with low cloud, heavy rain and fog, provided the setting for Conan Doyle's novel 'The Hound of the Baskervilles'. The heart of the moorland is crossed by only two significant roads meeting at Two Bridges, near Princetown with its infamous prison of 1806 the only town of any size. Remains of mining can be found at the Vitifer Tin Mine and the Wheal Betsy Pumping Engine House at Mary Tavy. Granite quarrying developed in the 19th century, the largest quarries were at Haytor and Fogginter (where stone for Nelson's Column in London was quarried).

The moor was extensively farmed in the bronze age when the climate was milder, and is covered in prehistoric remains such as the Merrivale Prehistoric Settlement, Grimspound near Postbridge and the remote Stall Moor and Butterdon stone rows. The moor has many medieval stone clapper bridges examples being at Postbridge, Bellever and Dartmeet.

The Ministry of Defence training area in the north part of the moor (with live firing- observe warning signs), has the two highest points of High Willhays (621 m, 2038 ft) and Yes Tor (619 m, 2030 ft). Other tors to the west of the moor are Great Staple Tor, Great Mis Tor and Vixen Tor, with a sphynx like profile, the tallest rock pile on Dartmoor at 27 m (90 ft) from base to top, near Merrivale. Hound Tor, with its deserted medieval village, the popular Haytor Rocks, with its granite tramway and Blackingstone Rock, 24 m (80 ft) above ground level with Victorian iron steps, are in the east.

There are many beauty spots in the river valleys around the edge of the moor. In the east is Fingle Bridge (near the famous Castle Drogo), Lustleigh Cleave, Becky Falls and Canonteign Falls near Hennock comprising Lady Exmouth Falls, at 67 m (220 ft) England's highest waterfall. In the west is Lydford Gorge and the more open Tavy Cleave. To the south is the Dewerstone Rock; the 50 m (165 ft) high crags form the finest rock climbing face in inland Devon. The granite 'chimney' Bowerman's Nose is near Manaton and the intriguing Ten Commandments Stone is at Buckland in the Moor.

MOORS

EXMOOR (see also Lynton and Lynmouth description)

Exmoor is mainly defined by the 267 square miles of the Exmoor National Park created in 1954. Comprising a plateau of sedimentary rocks and slate regularly reaching 400 m (1312 ft), it does not have the rugged granite tors of Bodmin Moor and Dartmoor, but is more remote and less crowded. The western edge rises sharply whilst the Brendon Hills to the east have the gentlest contours. The 30 square mile Exmoor Forest at Simonsbath (never in fact forested), were once a royal deer park. The area typifies the bleak upland moorland with coarse grass, bracken, heather and gorse especially seen at The Chains, a waterlogged wilderness forming the head waters of the Exe, Barle and West Lyn rivers.

Deep thickly wooded valleys make up the lower sections of the moor, many of which are accessible only by walking. Heddon's Cleave (200 m, 656 ft deep), is reached by footpath from Hunter's Inn, Badgworthy Water from Malmsmead, and Horner Wood (at 900 acre, one of the largest ancient oak woodlands in the country), by trails through the valley of Horner Water. Accessible by car is the National Trust owned Watersmeet, a popular beauty spot at the junction of the steep wooded valleys of the East Lyn River and Hoaroak Water east of Lynmouth.

There is spectacular scenery on the coast with a series of headlands interrupted only by the Vale of Porlock. Notable are the cliffs at Countisbury, at around 137 m (450 ft) the highest in Devon, and the striking Little Hangman near Combe Martin.

Exmoor is well known for large numbers of red deer and the native Exmoor ponies. Oare Church and Robber's Bridge are famous for their associations with R.D. Blackmore's novel 'Lorna Doone'. Doone Valley (actually Hoccombe Combe) is reached either by a 2 mile walk from Malmsmead along the valley of Badgworthy Water (which runs along the Devon Somerset border), or across Brendon Common.

Tarr Steps over the River Barle (at 55 m or 180 ft long with 17 spans), is the finest example of a clapper bridge in the country (best approached from the B3223 at Winsford Hill), Landacre Bridge is a preserved medieval bridge in a moorland setting near Withypool Common, whilst the scenic Bury Packhorse Bridge is near Dulverton. Exmoor's tallest standing stone, the 3 m (9 ft) high Longstone, and Chapman Barrows bronze age burial mounds, are near Challacombe. Dunkery Beacon at 519 m (1704 ft) is the highest point on Exmoor and in Somerset, whilst Western Common, near Kinsford Gate, at 493 m (1617 ft) is the highest point on Exmoor within Devon. From here, a desolate road follows the ridge along the Somerset border south east for 9 miles to West Anstey Common where the 13 ton Hancock Memorial Stone was erected in 1935 in memory of a local hunter. Other notable places are Culbone Church, near Porlock with its scenic toll roads, thought to be the smallest complete parish church in England and the town of Dunster, famous for its castle and gardens and early 17th century octagonal Yarn Market.

Portchapel Beach, Cornwall

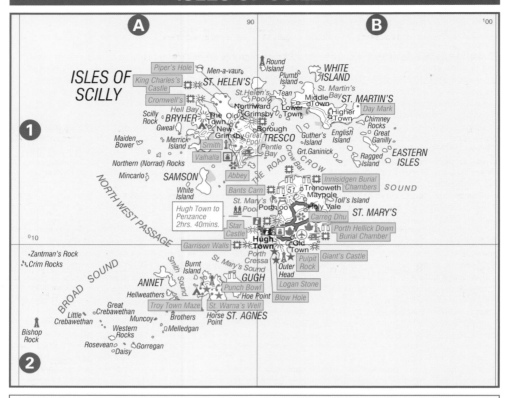

Tourist Information Centre (All year) - The Old Wesleyan Chapel, Garrison Lane, Hug Town, St Mary's.
Tel: 01720 422536

The Isles of Scilly, an archipelago of about 150 granite islands, islets and rocks, 28 miles south west of Land's End, are according to legend, the only visible relic of Lyonesse, the land of Arthurian legend. The islands have many bronze age cairns and iron age remains. With a very mild climate, the chief industry outside tourism is floriculture, with spring flowers grown in tiny sheltered fields being exported as early as November. The five largest islands are populated- St Mary's, Tresco, Bryher, St Martin's and St Agnes. Seals and seabirds abound on the many uninhabited islands and the autumn migration of both sea and land birds is renowned. Hug Town, St Mary's where launches leave to all the off islands, is reached by ferry and helicopter from Penzance and plane from Land's End Aerodrome (St Just).

St Mary's is the largest island with most of the population centred on the capital Hug Town, situated on the isthmus to The Garrison peninsula fortified by a 1.5 mile long granite wall punctuated with batteries, and Star Castle (now a hotel). The Isles of Scilly Museum is in Church Street and the Isles of Scilly Wildlife Trust Visitor Centre is on the Quay. To the north of the island are the bronze age Bant's Carn Burial Chamber and iron age Halangy Down Ancient Village; the best preserved bronze age burial mound being at Porth Hellick Down to the south. On the south coast Old Town Bay churchyard has the graves of 120 people lost in the wreck of the German trans-atlantic liner 'Schiller' in 1875 and Porth Hellick has a monument to Rear-Admiral Sir Cloudesley Shovell lost with the Association and three other ships in 1707 on the Western Rocks. Peninnis Head has the overhanging Pulpit Rock, Logan Stone weighing over 300 tons, and many naturally eroded granite shapes. Telegraph Hill is the highest point on St Mary's and Scilly at 51 m (167 ft).

Tresco is famous for its Tresco Abbey sub-tropical Gardens, on the site of a 12th century benedictine priory (of which an archway survives), and the Valhalla Collection of 19th century ships figureheads from vessels lost around the islands. The contrasting rugged north end of the island beyond New Grimsby has King Charles's Castle, the 17th century Cromwell's Castle, the Old Blockhouse harbour gun tower at Old Grimsby and Piper's Hole, a natural cave with pool.

Bryher is noted for the rocky coast at Shipman Head and Hell Bay on the wild northern part of the island.

St Martin's is known for its fine beaches on the south side. A large pepper pot navigation mark- the Day Mark of 1685, is on Chapel Down on the east tip. St Agnes has the Troy Town Maze on the Downs, set in pebbles by an 18th century keeper of St Agnes Lighthouse (built 1680 and disused in 1911), the second oldest surviving purpose built lighthouse in the country. Also of note is the the Punch Bowl, a curiously perched boulder on Wingletang Down. 4 miles south west, past the bird sanctuary on Annet, is Bishop Rock Lighthouse (built 1851-8 and rebuilt in 1883-7) one of Britain's tallest lighthouses guarding the treacherous waters around the Western Rocks, the scene of many shipwrecks.

(1) A strict alphabetical order is used e.g. Ash Thomas follows Ashrelghney but precedes Ashton.

(2) The map reference given refers to the actual map square in which the town spot or built-up area is located and not to the place name.

(3) Where two or more places of the same name occur in the same County or Unitary Authority, the nearest large town is also given;
e.g. Aish. *Devn* —1A **16** (nr. South Brent) indicates that Aish is located in square 1A on page **16** and is situated near South Brent in the County of Devon.

COUNTIES AND UNITARY AUTHORITIES with the abbreviations used in this index

Cornwall : *Corn*
Devon : *Devn*

Dorset : *Dors*
Isles of Scilly : *IOS*

North Somerset : *N Som*
Plymouth : *Plym*

Somerset : *Som*

INDEX

Cannington—Fair Oak

Cannington. Som —3C 37
Canonstown. Corn —2C 7
Canworthy Water. Corn —1A 20
Capton. Devn —2C 17
Capton. Som —3A 36
Caradon Town. Corn —3A 20
Carbis. Corn —2C 13
Carbis Bay. Corn —2C 7
Carclaze. Corn —2C 13
Carclew. Corn —1B 8
Cardinham. Corn —1D 13
Cardlidnack. Corn —2B 8
Cargreen. Corn —1C 15
Carhampton. Som —2A 36
Carharrack. Corn —3D 11
Carkeel. Corn —1C 15
Carleen. Corn —2D 7
Carlyon Bay. Corn —2C 13
Carn Brea Village. Corn —1D 7
Carne. Corn —2B 12
(nr. St Dennis)
Carne. Corn —1D 9
(nr. Veryan)
Carnhell Green. Corn —2D 7
Carnkie. Corn —2D 7
(nr. Camborne)
Carnkie. Corn —1B 8
(nr. Rame)
Carn Marth. Corn —3D 11
Carnon Downs. Corn —3D 11
Carn Towan. Corn —3A 6
Carnyorth. Corn —2A 6
Carpalla. Corn —2B 12
Carthew. Corn —2C 13
Castallack. Corn —3B 6
Castle Gate. Corn —2B 6
Catchall. Corn —3B 6
Catcott. Som —3D 37
Catherston Leweston. Dors —1D 25
Caton. Devn —3B 22
Cattedown Plym —2C 15
Caute. Devn —2C 27
Cawsand. Corn —2C 15
Chacewater. Corn —3D 11
Chaddlehanger. Devn —3C 21
Chaddlewood. Plym —2D 15
Chaffcombe. Som —2D 31
Challaborough. Devn —3A 16
Challacombe. Devn —2A 34
Chambercombe. Devn —2D 33
Champson. Devn —1C 29
Changford. Devn —2B 22
Chapel. Corn —1A 12
Chapel Allerton. Som —1D 37
Chapel Amble. Corn —3B 18
Chapel Cleeve. Som —2A 36
Chapel Leigh. Som —1B 30
Chapelton. Devn —1D 27
Chapel Town. Corn —2A 12
Chapmans Well. Devn —1B 20
Chard. Som —3D 31
Chard Junction. Som —3D 31
Chardleigh Green. Som —2D 31
Chardstock. Devn —3D 31
Charles. Devn —3A 34
Charles Bottom. Devn —3A 34
Charlestown. Corn —2C 13
Charlynch. Som —3C 37
Charmouth. Dors —1D 25
Chasty. Devn —3B 26
Chawleigh. Devn —2B 28
Cheddar. Som —1D 37
Cheddon Fitzpaine. Som —1C 31
Chedzoy. Som —3D 37
Cheglinch. Devn —2D 33
Cheldon. Devn —2B 28
Chelston. Som —1B 30
Chelston Torre. Devn —1C 17
Cheriton. Devn —2B 34
Cheriton Bishop. Devn —1B 22
Cheriton Cross. Devn —1B 22
Cherlton Fitzpaine. Devn —3C 29
Cherrybridge. Devn —2B 34
Cheston. Devn —2A 16
Chettiscombe. Devn —2D 29
Chevithorne. Devn —2D 29
Chichacott. Devn —1A 22
Chideock. Dors —1D 25
Chidgley. Som —3A 36
Chilla. Devn —3C 27
Chillaton. Devn —2C 21
Chillington. Devn —3B 16
Chillington. Som —2D 31
Chillsworthy. Devn —3B 26
Chilsworthy. Corn —3C 21
Chilton. Devn —3C 29
Chilton Polden. Som —3D 37
Chilton Trinity. Som —3C 37
Chipley. Som —1B 30
Chipstable. Som —1A 30
Chitterley. Devn —3D 29
Chittlehamholt. Devn —1A 28
Chivenor. Devn —3D 33
Christon. N Som —1D 37
Christow. Devn —2C 23
Chudleigh. Devn —3C 23
Chudleigh Knighton. Devn —3C 23
Chulmleigh. Devn —2A 28
Churchbridge. Corn —2A 14
Church Green. Devn —1B 24
Churchill. Devn —3C 31
(nr. Axminster)
Churchill. Devn —2D 33
(nr. Combe Martin)
Churchill. N Som —1D 37
Churchinford. Som —2C 31
Churchstanton. Som —2B 30
Churchstow. Devn —3B 16
Church Town. Corn —1D 7
(nr. Redruth)
Churchtown. Corn —3C 19
(nr. St Breward)
Churchtown. Devn —3A 26
(nr. Bridgerule)
Churchtown. Devn —2A 34
(nr. Parracombe)
Churscombe. Devn —1C 17
Churston Ferrers. Devn —2D 17
Chyandour. Corn —2B 6
Clapham. Devn —2C 23
Clapton. Som —3D 31
Clapworthy. Devn —1A 28
Clatworthy. Som —3A 36
Clavelshay. Som —3C 37
Clawton. Devn —1B 20
Clayhanger. Devn —1A 30
Clayhanger. Som —2D 31
Clayhidon. Devn —2B 30
Clearbrook. Devn —1D 15
Cleers. Corn —2B 12
Clewer. Som —1D 37
Cliff. Corn —2D 13
Clifton. Devn —2D 33
Clovelly. Devn —1B 26
Clyst Honiton. Devn —1D 23
Clyst Hydon. Devn —3A 30
Clyst St George. Devn —2D 23
Clyst St Lawrence. Devn —3A 30
Clyst St Mary. Devn —1D 23
Clyst William. Devn —3A 30
Coad's Green. Corn —3A 20
Coat. Som —1D 31
Cobbaton. Devn —1A 28
Cockington. Devn —1C 17
Cocklake. Som —2D 37
Cocks. Corn —2D 11
Cockwood. Devn —2D 23
Coffinswell. Devn —1C 17
Colan. Corn —1A 12
Colaton. Devn —2A 24
Coldeast. Devn —3C 23
Coldharbour. Corn —3D 11
Cold Northcott. Corn —2A 20
Coldridge. Devn —3A 28
Coldvreath. Corn —2B 12
Coldwind. Corn —1A 14
Colebrook. Devn —3A 30
Colebrooke. Devn —1B 22
Colestocks. Devn —3A 30
Collaton. Devn —3D 15
Collaton St Mary. Devn —1C 17
Collipreist. Devn —2D 29
Colliton. Devn —3A 30
Colscott. Devn —2B 26
Colyford. Devn —1C 25
Colyton. Devn —1C 25
Combebow. Devn —2C 21
Combe Fishacre. Devn —1C 17
Combe Florey. Som —3B 36
Combeinteignhead. Devn —3D 23
Combe Martin. Devn —2D 33
Combe Pafford. Devn —1D 17
Combe Raleigh. Devn —3B 30
Combe St Nicholas. Som —2D 31
Combpyne. Devn —1C 25
Combwich. Som —2C 37
Common Moor. Corn —1A 14
Compton. Devn —1C 17
Compton. Plym —2C 15
Compton Bishop. Som —1D 37
Congdon's Shop. Corn —3A 20
Congresbury. N Som —1D 37
Connor Downs. Corn —2C 7
Constantine. Corn —2B 8
Constantine Bay. Corn —3A 18
Cookbury. Devn —3C 27
Cookbury Wick. Devn —3B 26
Cooksland. Corn —1C 13
Coombe. Corn —2A 26
(nr. Kilkhampton)
Coombe. Corn —1D 7
(nr. Redruth)
Coombe. Corn —2B 12
(nr. St Stephen)
Coombe. Corn —3A 12
(nr. Truro)
Coombe. Devn —2A 30
(nr. Sampford Peverell)
Coombe. Devn —1B 24
(nr. Sidmouth)
Coombelake. Devn —1A 24
Coppathorne. Corn —3A 26
Copperhouse. Corn —2C 7
Corfe. Som —2C 31
Corndon. Devn —2A 22
Cornwood. Devn —2A 16
Cornworthy. Devn —2C 17
Coryton. Devn —2C 21
Cotford. Devn —1B 24
Cothelstone. Som —3B 36
Cotleigh. Devn —3C 31
Cotmanton. Devn —2B 24
Cott. Devn —1B 16
Cotts. Devn —1C 15
Cotteylands. Devn —2D 29
Couch's Mill. Corn —2D 13
Coultings. Som —2C 37
Countess Wear. Devn —2D 23
Countisbury. Devn —2B 34
Courtway. Som —3C 37
Cove. Devn —2D 29
Coverack. Corn —3B 8
Coverack Bridges. Corn —2D 7
Cowlands. Corn —3A 12
Cowley. Devn —1D 23
Cowleymoor. Devn —2D 29
Crackington Haven. Corn —1D 19
Craddock. Devn —2A 30
Crafthole. Corn —2B 14
Cranford. Devn —1B 26
Crantock. Corn —1D 11
Crapstone. Devn —1D 15
Crawley. Devn —3C 31
Creach Heathfield. Som —1C 31
Creach St Michael. Som —1C 31
Creacombe. Devn —2C 29
Crediton. Devn —3C 29
Creed. Corn —3B 12
Creegbrawse. Corn —3D 11
Cremyll. Corn —2C 15
Crewkerne. Som —3D 31
Cricket Malherbie. Som —2D 31
Cricket St Thomas. Som —3D 31
Crickham. Som —2D 37
Criggan. Corn —1C 13
Crimchard. Som —3D 31
Crimp. Corn —2A 26
Cripplesease. Corn —2C 7
Croanford. Corn —3C 19
Crockemwell. Devn —1B 22
Croford. Som —1B 30
Crofthandy Corn —3D 11
Cross. Devn —3C 33
Cross. Som —1D 37
Cross Coombe. Corn —2D 11
Cross Green. Devn —2B 20
Crossington. Som —2D 37
Cross Lanes. Corn —3D 7
Cross Side. Devn —1C 29
Crowan. Corn —2D 7
Crowcombe. Som —3B 36
Crowden. Devn —1C 21
Crowlas. Corn —2C 7
Crownhill. Plym —2C 15
Crowntown. Corn —2D 7
Crows-an-wra. Corn —3A 6
Crow's Nest. Corn —1A 14
Croyde. Devn —3C 33
Croyde Bay. Devn —3C 33
Cruft. Devn —1D 21
Crugmeer. Corn —3B 18
Crumplehorn. Corn —2A 14
Cruwys Morchard. Devn —2C 29
Cubert. Corn —2D 11
Cudlipptown. Devn —3D 21
Cudworth. Som —2D 31
Cullaford. Devn —1A 22
Cullompton. Devn —3A 30
Culm Davy. Devn —2B 30
Culmstock. Devn —2B 30
Culver. Devn —1C 23
Culverlane. Devn —1B 16
Curland. Som —2C 31
Currian Vale. Corn —2B 12
Curry Mallet. Som —1D 31
Curry Rivel. Som —1D 31
Curtisknowle. Devn —2B 16
Cury. Corn —3D 7
Cusgarne. Corn —3D 11
Cutcombe. Som —3D 35
Cutmadoc. Corn —1C 13
Cutmere. Corn —1B 14
Cuttivett. Corn —1B 14

Daccombe. Devn —1D 17
Dainton. Devn —1C 17
Dalwood. Devn —3C 31
Darite. Corn —1A 14
Darleyford. Corn —3A 20
Darracott. Devn —3C 33
(nr. Croyde)
Darracott. Devn —2A 26
(nr. Welcombe)
Dartington. Devn —1B 16
Dartmeet. Devn —3A 22
Dartmouth. Devn —2C 17
Davidstow. Corn —2D 19
Dawlish. Devn —3D 23
Dawlish Warren. Devn —3D 23
Daw's Green. Som —1B 30
Daw's House. Corn —2B 20
Dean. Devn —2A 34
(nr. Combe Martin)
Dean. Devn —2B 34
(nr. Lynton)
Dean Cross. Devn —2D 33
Dean Prior. Devn —1B 16
Delabole. Corn —2C 19
Demelza. Corn —1B 12
Denbury. Devn —1C 17
Derriton. Devn —3B 26
Devonport. Plym —2C 15
Devoran. Corn —1B 8
Dexbeer. Devn —3A 26
Didworthy. Devn —1A 16
Dinas. Corn —3B 18
Dinnington. Som —2D 31
Dinworthy. Devn —2B 26
Dippertown. Devn —2C 21
Dipple. Devn —2B 26
Diptford. Devn —2B 16
Dittisham. Devn —2C 17
Dizzard. Corn —1D 19
Dobwalls. Corn —1A 14
Doccombe. Devn —2B 22
Doddiscombsleigh. Devn —2C 23
Doddycross. Corn —1B 14
Dodington. Som —2B 36
Dog Village. Devn —1D 23
Dolton. Devn —2D 27
Doniford. Som —2A 36
Donyatt. Som —2D 31
Doublebois. Corn —1D 13
Dousland. Devn —1D 15
Dowland. Devn —2D 27
Dowlands. Devn —1C 25
Dowlish Ford. Som —2D 31
Dowlish Wake. Som —2D 31
Downderry. Corn —2B 14
(nr. Seaton)
Downderry. Corn —2B 12
(nr. St Stephen)
Downgate. Corn —3B 20
(nr. Kelly Bray)
Downgate. Corn —3A 20
(nr. Pensilva)
Downicary. Devn —1B 20
Down St Mary. Devn —3B 28
Down Thomas. Devn —2D 15
Drakeland Corner. Devn —2D 15
Drakewalls. Corn —3C 21
Drayford. Devn —2B 28
Draynes. Corn —1A 14
Drayton. Som —1D 31
Drewsteignton. Devn —1B 22
Drift. Corn —3B 6
Drimpton. Dors —3D 31
Drym. Corn —2D 7
Duddlestone. Som —1C 31
Dulford. Devn —3A 30
Duloe. Corn —2A 14
Dulverton. Som —1D 29
Dumpinghill. Devn —3C 27
Dunball. Som —2D 37
Dunchideock. Devn —2C 23
Dunkeswell. Devn —3B 30
Dunmere. Corn —1C 13
Dunsford. Devn —2C 23
Dunster. Som —2D 35
Dunstone. Devn —3B 22
(nr. Ashburton)
Dunstone. Devn —2D 15
(nr. Yealmpton)
Duporth. Corn —2C 13
Durgan. Corn —2B 8
Durleigh. Som —3C 37
Durston. Som —1C 31
Dutson. Corn —2B 20

Eastacombe. Devn —1D 27
Eastacott. Corn —2A 26
East Allington. Devn —3B 16
East Anstey Devn —1C 29
East Ashley. Devn —2A 28
East Brent. Som —1D 37
East Buckland. Devn —3A 34
East Budleigh. Devn —2A 24
East Butterleigh. Devn —3D 29
East Charleton. Devn —3B 16
East Combe. Som —3B 36
East Cornworthy. Devn —2C 17
Eastcott. Devn —2C 21
East Down. Devn —2A 34
Eastertown. Som —1D 37
East Huntspill. Som —2D 37
East Illkerton. Devn —2B 34
Eastington. Devn —3B 28
East Kimber. Devn —1C 21
East Knowstone. Devn —1C 29
East Lambrook. Som —2D 31
Eastleigh. Devn —1C 27
(nr. Bideford)
East Leigh. Devn —2A 16
(nr. Modbury)
East Leigh. Devn —3A 28
(nr. North Tawton)
East Lydeard. Som —1B 30
East Nynehead. Som —1B 30
East Ogwell. Devn —3C 23
Easton. Devn —2B 22
East Panson. Devn —1B 20
East Putford. Devn —2B 26
East Quantoxhead. Som —2B 36
East Stowford. Devn —1A 28
East Taphouse. Corn —1D 13
East-the-Water. Devn —1C 27
East Village. Devn —3C 29
East Week. Devn —1A 22
East Westacott. Devn —2D 27
East Worlington. Devn —2B 28
East Youlstone. Devn —2A 26
Ebberley Hill. Devn —2D 27
Ebford. Devn —2D 23
Ebsworthy. Devn —1D 21
Edgcott. Som —3C 35
Edgecumbe. Corn —1B 8
Edginswell. Devn —1C 17
Edington. Som —2D 37
Edingworth. Som —1D 37
Edistone. Devn —1A 26
Edithmead. Som —2D 37
Edmonton. Corn —3B 18
Efford. Devn —3C 29
Eggbuckland. Plym —2C 15
Eggesford. Devn —2A 28
Eggesford Barton. Devn —2A 28
Egloshayle. Corn —3C 19
Egloskerry. Corn —2A 20
Elburton. Plym —2D 15
Ellbridge. Corn —1C 15
Ellerhayes. Devn —3D 29
Elmscott. Devn —1A 26
Elsford. Devn —2B 22
Elston. Devn —3B 28
Elworth. Som —3A 36
Enmore. Som —3C 37
Enniscaven. Corn —2B 12
Ermington. Devn —2A 16
Ernesettle. Plym —2C 15
Escalls. Corn —3A 6
Escott. Som —3A 36
Estover. Plym —2D 15
Eworthy. Devn —1C 21
Exbourne. Devn —3A 28
Exebridge. Som —1D 29
Exeter. Devn —1D 23
Exford. Som —3C 35
Exmansworthy. Devn —1A 26
Exminster. Devn —2D 23
Exmouth. Devn —2A 24
Exton. Devn —2D 23
Exton. Som —3D 35

Fairmile. Devn —1A 24
Fair Oak. Devn —2A 30

68 Visitors' Devon & Cornwall Atlas

Fairy Cross—Knowle

Fairy Cross. Devn —1C 27
Falmouth. Corn —1B 8
Farms Common. Corn —2D 7
Farringdon. Devn —1A 24
Farringdon Cross. Devn —1A 24
Farway. Devn —1B 24
Fawton. Corn —1D 13
Feniton. Devn —1A 24
Fenny Bridges. Devn —1B 24
Feock. Corn —1C 9
Fernsplatt. Corn —3D 11
Fiddington. Som —2C 37
Fiddlers Green. Corn —2A 12
Filford. Dors —1D 25
Filleigh. Devn —2B 28
(nr. Lapford)
Filleigh. Devn —1A 28
(nr. Swimbridge)
Finnington. Som —1B 30
Fishpond Bottom. Dors —1D 25
Fitzhead. Som —1B 30
Fitzroy. Som —1B 30
Five Bells. Som —2A 36
Fivehead. Som —1D 31
Fivelanes. Corn —2A 20
Flaxpool. Som —3B 36
Fletchersbridge. Corn —1D 13
Flexbury. Corn —3A 26
Flushing. Corn —2B 8
(nr. Mannaccan)
Flushing. Corn —1C 9
(nr. Penryn)
Fluxton. Devn —1A 24
Folly Cross. Devn —3C 27
Folly Gate. Devn —1D 21
Fonston. Corn —1A 20
Ford. Devn —3B 16
(nr. Chillington)
Ford. Devn —1C 27
(nr. Saltrens)
Ford. Plym —2C 15
Ford. Som —1A 30
Forda. Corn —2A 26
Forda. Devn —3C 33
Ford Barton. Devn —2D 29
Forder Green. Devn —1B 16
Fordgate. Som —3D 37
Ford Street. Som —2B 30
Fordton. Devn —1C 23
Forge. Corn —1D 7
Fort Hill. Devn —3D 33
Forton. Som —3D 31
Four Cross Way. Devn —3A 34
Four Forks. Som —3C 37
Four Lane. Corn —2D 7
Fowey. Corn —2D 13
Foxhole. Corn —2B 12
Fraddam. Corn —2C 7
Fraddon. Corn —2B 12
Freathy. Corn —2B 14
Fremington. Devn —3D 33
Frenchbeer. Devn —2A 22
Frithelstock. Devn —2C 27
Frithelstock Stone. Devn —2C 27
Frittiscombe. Devn —3C 17
Frogmore. Devn —3B 16
Frogpool. Corn —3D 11
Frogwell. Corn —1B 14
Fulford. Som —1C 31
Fulwood. Som —1C 31
Furley. Devn —3C 31
Furzehill. Devn —2B 34

Galmington. Som —1C 31
Galmpton. Devn —2C 17
(nr. Brixham)
Galmpton. Devn —3A 16
(nr. Malborough)
Gammaton. Devn —1C 27
Gammaton Moor. Devn —1C 27
Gang. Corn —1B 14
Gappah. Devn —3C 23
Garker. Corn —2C 13
Garlandhayes. Devn —2B 30
Garras. Corn —2B 8
Gear Sands. Corn —2D 11
Georgeham. Devn —3C 33
George Nympton. Devn —1A 28
Germansweek. Devn —1C 21
Germoe. Corn —3C 7
Gerrans. Corn —1C 9
Gidleigh. Devn —2A 22
Gilbert's Coombe. Corn —1D 7
Gillan. Corn —2B 8
Gittisham. Devn —1B 24
Gluvian. Corn —1B 12
Goathurst. Som —3C 37
Godford Cross. Devn —3B 30
Godolphin Cross. Corn —2D 7
Golant. Corn —2D 13
Golberdon. Corn —3B 20
Goldsithney. Corn —2C 7
Goldworthy. Devn —1B 26
Goodrington. Devn —2C 17
Goodstone. Devn —3B 22
Goonbell. Corn —3D 11
Goonhavern. Corn —2D 11
Goonpiper. Corn —1C 9
Goonvrea. Corn —3D 11
Gooseford. Devn —1A 22
Gooseham. Corn —2A 26
Goosemoor. Devn —2A 24
Goosewell. Devn —2D 33
Gorran Churchtown. Corn —3C 13
Gorran Haven. Corn —3C 13
Gorran High Lanes. Corn —3B 12
Gothers. Corn —2B 12
Goveton. Devn —3B 16
Gracca. Corn —2C 13
Grade. Corn —3B 8
Grampound. Corn —3B 12
Grampound Road. Corn —2B 12
Gratton. Devn —2B 26
Great Bosullow. Corn —2B 6
Great Potheridge. Devn —2D 27
Great Torr. Devn —3A 16
Great Torrington. Devn —2C 27
Great Tree. Corn —2A 14
Green Bottom. Corn —3D 11
Greenham. Dors —3D 31
Greenham. Som —1A 30
Greensplat. Corn —2B 12
Greinton. Som —3D 37
Grenofen. Devn —3C 21
Greylake. Som —3D 37
Grimscott. Corn —3A 26
Grinacombe Moor. Devn —1C 21
Grindhill. Devn —1C 21
Grumbla. Corn —3B 6
Guineaford. Devn —3D 33
Gulval. Corn —2B 6
Gulvian. Corn —1A 12
Gummow's Shop. Corn —2A 12
Gunn. Devn —3A 34
Gunnislake. Corn —3C 21
Gunwalloe. Corn —3D 7
Gupworthy. Som —3D 35
Gweek. Corn —2B 8
Gwennap. Corn —3D 11
Gwenter. Corn —3B 8
Gwills. Corn —2A 12
Gwindra. Corn —2B 12
Gwinear. Corn —2C 7
Gwithian. Corn —1C 7

Haggington Hill. Devn —2D 33
Hakeford. Devn —3A 34
Halabezack. Corn —1B 8
Halberton. Devn —2A 30
Half Moon Village. Devn —1C 23
Halford. Devn —3C 23
Halgabron. Corn —2C 19
Hallane. Corn —3C 13
Hallew. Corn —2C 13
Hallspill. Devn —1C 27
Hallworthy. Corn —2D 19
Halsetown. Corn —2C 7
Halsfordwood. Devn —1C 23
Halsinger. Devn —3D 33
Halstow. Devn —1C 23
Halsway. Som —3B 36
Halwell. Devn —2B 16
Halwill. Devn —1C 21
Halwill Junction. Devn —1C 21
Ham. Devn —3C 31
Ham. Plym —2C 15
Ham. Som —1C 31
(nr. Creech St Michael)
Ham. Som —2C 31
(nr. Horton)
Hambridge. Som —1D 31
Hamlet. Devn —1B 24
Hamp. Som —3C 37
Hampt. Corn —3B 20
Hampton. Devn —1C 25
Hand and Pen. Devn —1A 24
Hannaborough. Devn —3D 27
Hannaford. Devn —1A 28
Harberton. Devn —2B 16
Harbertonford. Devn —2B 16
Harbourneford. Devn —1B 16
Harcombe. Devn —1B 24
(nr. Sidford)
Harcombe. Devn —2C 23
(nr. Trusham)
Harcombe Bottom. Devn —1D 25
Harford. Devn —2A 16
Harleston. Devn —3B 16
Harpford. Devn —1A 24
Harracott. Devn —1D 27
Harrowbarrow. Corn —3B 20
Harrowbeer. Devn —1D 15
Hartland. Devn —1A 26
Hartland Quay. Devn —1A 26
Hartswell. Som —1A 30
Hartyn. Corn —3A 18
Hatch Beauchamp. Som —1D 31
Hatch Green. Som —2C 31
Hatherleigh. Devn —3D 27
Hatt. Corn —1B 14
Hawkchurch. Devn —3D 31
Hawkcombe. Som —2C 35
Hawkerland. Devn —2A 24
Hawkridge. Som —3C 35
Haydon. Som —1C 31
Haye. Corn —1B 14
Hayle. Corn —2C 7
Hayne. Devn —3C 29
Haytor Vale. Devn —3B 22
Haytown. Devn —2B 26
Hazelwood. Devn —2B 16
(nr. Loddiswell)
Hazelwood. Devn —2C 23
(nr. Trusham)
Heale. Devn —2A 34
Heamoor. Corn —2B 6
Heanton Punchardon. Devn —3D 33
Heasley Mill. Devn —3B 34
Heath Cross. Devn —1A 22
Heathercombe. Devn —2B 22
Heathfield. Devn —3C 23
Heathfield. Som —1B 30
Heath House. Som —2D 37
Heathstock. Devn —3C 31
Heavitree. Devn —1D 23
Heddon. Devn —1A 28
Hedging. Som —1C 31
Hele. Devn —3B 22
(nr. Ashburton)
Hele. Devn —1B 20
(nr. Boyton)
Hele. Devn —3D 29
(nr. Bradninch)
Hele. Devn —2D 33
(nr. Ilfracombe)
Hele. Som —1B 30
Helford. Corn —2B 8
Helford Passage. Corn —2B 8
Helland. Corn —3C 19
Helland. Som —1D 31
Hellandbridge. Corn —3C 19
Hellescott. Corn —2A 20
Hellesveor. Corn —1C 7
Helston. Corn —3D 7
Helstone. Corn —2C 19
Helstone Water. Corn —3D 11
Hemerdon. Devn —2D 15
Hemsford. Devn —1C 17
Hemyock. Devn —2B 30
Hendra. Corn —2B 12
(nr. St Dennis)
Hendra. Corn —2C 19
(nr. St Teath)
Hendra. Corn —1B 8
(nr. Stithians)
Hendrabridge. Corn —1A 14
Hendra Croft. Corn —2D 11
Henford. Devn —1B 20
Henlade. Som —1C 31
Henley. Som —3D 37
Hennock. Devn —2C 23
Henstridge. Devn —2D 33
Henwood. Corn —3A 20
Herner. Devn —1D 27
Herodsfoot. Corn —1A 14
Hersham. Corn —3A 26
Hessenford. Corn —2B 14
Hewas Water. Corn —3B 12
Hewish. Som —3D 31
Hexworthy. Devn —3A 22
Heybrook Bay. Devn —3C 15
Highampton. Devn —3C 27
High Bickington. Devn —1A 28
High Bray. Devn —3A 34
Highbridge. Som —2D 37
High Bullen. Devn —1D 27
High Cross. Corn —2B 8
Higher Ashton. Devn —2C 23
Higher Bal. Corn —2D 11
Higher Boscaswell. Corn —2A 6
Higher Cheriton. Devn —3B 30
Higher Chieflowman. Devn —2A 30
Higher Clovelly. Devn —1B 26
Higher Condurrow. Corn —2D 7
Higher Gabwell. Devn —1D 17
Higher Godsworthy. Devn —3D 21
Higher Harlyn. Corn —3A 18
Higher Muddiford. Devn —3D 33
Higher Porthpean. Corn —2C 13
Higher Slade. Devn —2D 33
Higher Tale. Devn —3A 30
Highertown. Corn —2D 19
(nr. Camelford)
Highertown. Corn —3A 12
(nr. Truro)
Higher Town. IOS —1B 66
Higher Town. Som —2D 35
Higher Tremarcoombe. Corn —1A 14
Higher Whitleigh. Corn —1A 20
High Ham. Som —3D 37
High Street. Corn —2B 12
Highweek. Devn —3C 23
Highworthy. Devn —3C 27
Hillcommon. Som —1B 30
Hillerton. Devn —1B 22
Hillfarrance. Som —1B 30
Hillfield. Devn —2C 17
Hillhead. Devn —2D 17
Hillsborough. Devn —2D 33
Hillside. Devn —1B 16
Hilltown. Devn —1B 28
Hinton St George. Som —2D 31
Hiscott. Devn —1D 27
Hittisleigh. Devn —1B 22
Hittisleigh Barton. Devn —1B 22
Hockworthy. Devn —2A 30
Hoe, The. Plym —2C 15
Holbeton. Devn —2A 16
Holcombe. Devn —1D 25
(nr. Lyme Regis)
Holcombe. Devn —3D 23
(nr. Teignmouth)
Holcombe Rogus. Devn —2A 30
Holditch. Dors —3D 31
Holdsworthy Beacon. Devn —3B 26
Holemoor. Devn —3C 27
Holewater. Devn —3B 34
Holford. Som —2B 36
Hollacombe. Devn —3B 26
Hollocombe. Devn —2A 28
Hollocombe Town. Devn —2A 28
Hollywell Lake. Som —1B 30
Holmacott. Devn —1D 27
Holman Clavel. Som —2C 31
Holmbush. Corn —2C 13
Holne. Devn —1B 16
Holsworthy. Devn —3B 26
Holwood. Corn —1B 14
Holy Vale. IOS —1B 66
Holywell. Corn —2D 11
Honeychurch. Devn —3A 28
Honiton. Devn —3B 30
Hooe. Plym —2D 15
Hookway. Devn —1C 23
Hoo Meavy. Devn —1D 15
Horndon. Devn —3D 21
Horner. Som —2C 35
Hornick. Corn —2B 12
Horningtops. Corn —1A 14
Horns Cross. Devn —1B 26
Horrabridge. Devn —1D 15
Horsebridge. Corn —3C 21
Horsebrook. Devn —2B 16
Horsey. Som —3D 37
Horton. Som —2D 31
Horton Cross. Som —2D 31
Horwood. Devn —1D 27
Houndsmoor. Som —1B 30
Howleigh. Som —2C 31
Howley. Som —3C 31
Huccaby. Devn —3A 22
Huddisford. Devn —2B 26
Hugh Town. IOS —1B 66
Hugus. Corn —3D 11
Huish Champflower. Som —1A 30
Huish Episcopi. Som —1D 31
Hulham. Devn —2A 24
Humber. Devn —3C 23
Hungerford. Som —2A 36
Huntham. Som —1D 31
Huntscott. Som —2D 35
Huntsham. Devn —1A 30
Huntshaw. Devn —1D 27
Huntshaw Water. Devn —1D 27
Huntspill. Som —2D 37
Huntstile. Som —3C 37
Huntworth. Som —3D 37
Hurcott. Som —2D 31
Hursey. Dors —3D 31
Hurston. Devn —2A 22
Hutcherleigh. Devn —2B 16
Hutton. N Som —1D 37
Huxham. Devn —1D 23

Iddesleigh. Devn —3D 27
Ide. Devn —1C 23
Ideford. Devn —3C 23
Idless. Corn —3A 12
Ilford. Som —2D 31
Ilfracombe. Devn —2D 33
Illogan. Corn —1D 7
Ilminster. Som —2D 31
Ilton. Som —2D 31
Indian Queens. Corn —2B 12
Indicott. Devn —2D 33
Ingleigh Green. Devn —3A 28
Instow. Devn —3C 33
Insworke. Corn —2C 15
Inwardleigh. Devn —1D 21
Ipplepen. Devn —1C 17
Isle Abbotts. Som —1D 31
Isle Brewers. Som —1D 31
Itton. Devn —1A 22
Ivybridge. Devn —2A 16

Jack-in-the-Green. Devn —1A 24
Jacobstow. Corn —1D 19
Jacobstowe. Devn —3D 27
Jurston. Devn —2A 22

Kea. Corn —3A 12
Keason. Corn —1B 14
Keaton. Devn —2A 16
Kehelland. Corn —1D 7
Kellacott. Devn —2C 21
Kelly. Devn —2B 20
Kelly Bray. Corn —3B 20
Kelynack. Corn —3A 6
Kemacott. Devn —2A 34
Kenn. Devn —2D 23
Kenneggy Downs. Corn —3C 7
Kennerleigh. Devn —3C 29
Kennford. Devn —2D 23
Kentisbeare. Devn —3A 30
Kentisbury. Devn —2A 34
Kentisbury Ford. Devn —2A 34
Kenton. Devn —2D 23
Kenwyn. Corn —3A 12
Kernborough. Devn —3B 16
Kerris. Corn —3B 6
Kerswell. Devn —3A 30
Kerthen Wood. Corn —2C 7
Kestle Mill. Corn —2A 12
Kewstoke. N Som —1D 37
Kilkhampton. Corn —2A 26
Killington. Devn —2A 34
Kilmington. Devn —1C 25
Kilton. Som —2B 36
Kilve. Som —2B 36
Kingford. Devn —2A 28
Kingsand. Corn —2C 15
Kingsbridge. Devn —3B 16
Kingsbridge. Som —3D 35
Kingsbury Episcopi. Som —1D 31
Kingscott. Devn —2D 27
Kingsdon. Devn —1C 25
Kingskerswell. Devn —1C 17
Kingsteignton. Devn —3C 23
Kingston. Devn —2A 24
(nr. Colaton Raleigh)
Kingston. Devn —2D 17
(nr. Kingswear)
Kingston. Devn —3A 16
(nr. Ringmore)
Kingstone. Som —2D 31
Kingston St Mary. Som —1C 31
Kingswear. Devn —2C 17
Kingswood. Som —3B 36
Kittisford. Som —1A 30
Kittisford Barton. Som —1A 30
Knapp. Som —1D 31
Knightacott. Devn —3A 34
Knightcott. N Som —1D 37
Knighton. Devn —3D 15
Knighton. Som —2B 36
Knowle. Devn —1B 16
(nr. Ashburton)

Knowle—Noss Mayo

Knowle. Devn —3C 33
(nr. Braunton)
Knowle. Devn —3A 30
(nr. Collompton)
Knowle. Devn —3B 28
(nr. Copplestone)
Knowle. Devn —2A 24
(nr. Exmouth)
Knowle Cross. Devn —1A 24
Knowle St Giles. Som —2D 31
Knowstone. Devn —1C 29
Kuggar. Corn —3B 8

Ladock. Corn —2A 12
Ladycross. Corn —2B 20
Lake. Devn —3D 33
(nr. Barnstaple)
Lake. Devn —3C 27
(nr. Chilla)
Lamellion. Corn —1A 14
Lamerton. Devn —3C 21
Lamorick. Corn —1C 13
Lamorna. Corn —3B 6
Lamorran. Corn —3A 12
Lampen. Corn —1D 13
Lana. Devn —1B 20
(nr. Nethercott)
Lana. Devn —3B 26
(nr. Pancrasweek)
Lanarth. Corn —2B 8
Landcross. Devn —1C 27
Landkey. Devn —3D 33
Landkey Newland. Devn —3D 33
Landrake. Corn —1B 14
Landscove. Devn —1B 16
Landulph. Corn —1C 15
Lane. Corn —1A 12
Laneast. Corn —2A 20
Langaford. Devn —1C 21
Langarth. Corn —3D 11
Langdon. Corn —1A 20
Langdon Cross. Corn —2B 20
Langford. Devn —1D 23
(nr. Exeter)
Langford. Devn —3A 30
(nr. Plymtree)
Langford Barton. Corn —3A 26
Langford Barton. Devn —2A 16
Langley. Som —1A 30
Langley Marsh. Som —1A 30
Langore. Corn —2A 20
Langport. Som —1D 31
Langridgeford. Devn —1D 27
Langtree. Devn —2C 27
Lanivet. Corn —1C 13
Lanjeth. Corn —2B 12
Lank. Corn —3C 19
Lanlivery. Corn —2C 13
Lanner. Corn —1B 8
Lanreath. Corn —2D 13
Lansallos. Corn —2D 13
Lanteglos Highway. Corn —2D 13
Lanvean. Corn —1A 12
Lapford. Devn —3B 28
Larkbeare. Devn —1A 24
Larrick. Corn —3B 20
Latchley. Corn —3C 21
Laughton Budville. Som —1B 30
Launcells Cross. Corn —3A 26
Launceston. Corn —2B 20
Lawhitton. Corn —2B 20
Laymore. Dors —3D 31
Ledstone. Devn —3B 16
Lee. Devn —2C 33
(nr. Ilfracombe)
Lee. Devn —1C 29
(nr. Molland)
Leedstown. Corn —2D 7
Leeford. Devn —2B 34
Lee Mill. Devn —2D 15
Lee Moor. Devn —1D 15
Leigham. Plym —2D 15
Leighland Chapel. Som —3A 36
Lelant. Corn —2C 7
Lelant Downs. Corn —2C 7
Lerryn. Corn —2D 13
Lesnewth. Corn —1D 19
Lettaford. Devn —2B 22
Leusdon. Devn —3B 22
Levalsa Meor. Corn —3C 13
Lewannick. Corn —2A 20
Lewdon. Devn —2C 21
Leworthy. Devn —3A 34
(nr. Bratton Fleming)
Leworthy. Devn —3B 26
(nr. Holsworthy)
Lewthorn Cross. Devn —3B 22
Lewtrenchard. Devn —2C 21
Ley. Corn —1D 13
Lezant. Corn —3B 20
Lezerea. Corn —2D 7
Lidwell. Corn —3B 20
Lifton. Devn —2B 20
Liftondown. Devn —2B 20
Lilstock. Som —2B 36
Linkinhorne. Corn —3B 20
Liscombe. Som —3C 35
Liskeard. Corn —1A 14
Little Comfort. Corn —2B 20
Little Croft West. Corn —3D 11
Littleham. Devn —2A 24
(nr. Exmouth)
Littleham. Devn —1C 27
(nr. Saltrens)
Littlehampton. Devn —1C 17
Little Petherick. Corn —3B 18
Little Potheridge. Devn —2D 27
Little Silver. Devn —3D 29
Little Torrington. Devn —2C 27
Littlewindsor. Dors —3D 31
Liverton. Devn —3C 23
Livingshayes. Devn —3D 29
Lizard. Corn —3B 8
Llsington. Devn —3B 22
Lobb. Devn —3C 33
Lobhillcross. Devn —2C 21
Lockengate. Corn —1C 13
Locking. N Som —1D 37
Loddiswell. Devn —3B 16
London Apprentice. Corn —2C 13
Longbridge. Plym —2D 15
Longcombe. Devn —2C 17
Longdown. Devn —1C 23
Longdowns. Corn —1B 8
Longrock. Corn —2C 7
Longstone. Corn —3C 19
Looe. Corn —2A 14
Lopen. Som —2D 31
Lostwithiel. Corn —2D 13
Lower Amble. Corn —3B 18
Lower Ashton. Devn —2C 23
Lower Boscaswell. Corn —2A 6
Lower Cheriton. Devn —3B 30
Lower Dean. Devn —1B 16
Lower Eype. Dors —1D 25
Lower Gabwell. Devn —1D 17
Lower Godsworthy. Devn —3D 21
Lower Lanherne. Corn —1A 12
Lower Lovacott. Devn —1D 27
Lower Loxhore. Devn —3A 34
Lower Roadwater. Som —3A 36
Lower Slade. Devn —2D 33
Lower Tale. Devn —3A 30
Lowertown. Corn —3D 7
Lower Town. Devn —3B 22
(nr. Ashburton)
Lowertown. Devn —2C 21
(nr. Stowford)
Lower Town. IOS —1B 66
Lower Twitchen. Devn —2B 26
Lower Vexford. Som —3B 36
Lower Weare. Som —1D 37
Lower Yelland. Devn —3C 33
Low Ham. Som —1D 31
Lowton. Devn —3A 28
Lowton. Som —2B 30
Loxbeare. Devn —2D 29
Loxhore. Devn —3A 34
Loxton. N Som —1D 37
Luccombe. Som —2D 35
Luckett. Corn —3B 20
Luckwell Bridge. Som —3D 35
Ludgvan. Corn —2C 7
Luffincott. Devn —1B 20
Luppitt. Devn —3B 30
Lupridge. Devn —2B 16
Luscombe. Devn —2B 16
Luson. Devn —2A 16
Lustleigh. Devn —2B 22
Luton. Devn —3D 23
(nr. Ideford)
Luton. Devn —3A 30
(nr. Payhembury)
Lutsford. Devn —2A 26
Lutton. Devn —2D 15
(nr. Cornwood)
Lutton. Devn —1A 16
(nr. South Brent)
Lutworthy. Devn —2B 28
Luxborough. Som —3D 35
Luxulyan. Corn —2C 13
Lydcott. Devn —3A 34
Lydeard St Lawrence. Som —3B 36
Lydford. Devn —2D 21
Lydmarsh. Som —3D 31
Lyme Regis. Dors —1D 25
Lympsham. Som —1D 37
Lympstone. Devn —2D 23
Lynbridge. Devn —2B 34
Lynch. Som —2D 35
Lyng. Som —1D 31
Lynmouth. Devn —2B 34
Lynstone. Corn —3A 26
Lynton. Devn —2B 34

Mabe Burnthouse. Corn —1B 8
Maddaford. Devn —1D 21
Maders. Corn —3B 20
Madford. Devn —2B 30
Madron. Corn —2B 6
Maenporth. Corn —2B 8
Maer. Corn —3A 26
Maidenwell. Corn —3D 19
Maldencombe. Devn —1D 17
Malmsmead. Devn —2B 34
Malpass. Corn —3A 12
Manaccan. Corn —2B 8
Manaton. Devn —2B 22
Manley. Devn —2D 29
Marazanvose. Corn —2D 11
Marazion. Corn —2C 7
Marhamchurch. Corn —3A 26
Mariansleigh. Devn —1B 28
Maristow. Devn —1C 15
Mark. Som —2D 37
Mark Causeway. Som —2D 37
Markwell. Corn —2B 14
Marldon. Devn —1C 17
Marsh. Devn —2C 31
Marshalsea. Dors —3D 31
Marsh Barton. Devn —1D 23
Marshgate. Corn —1D 19
Marsh Green. Devn —1A 24
Marsh Street. Som —2D 35
Marshwood. Dors —1D 25
Martinhoe. Devn —2A 34
Martinhoe Cross. Devn —2A 34
Marwood. Devn —3D 33
Marystow. Devn —2C 21
Mary Tavy. Devn —3D 21
Mawgan. Corn —2B 8
Mawgan Porth. Corn —1A 12
Mawla. Corn —3D 11
Mawnan. Corn —2B 8
Mawnan Smith. Corn —2B 8
Maxworthy. Corn —1A 20
Mayfield. Corn —2C 15
Mayon. Corn —3A 6
Maypole. IOS —1B 66
Mead. Devn —2A 26
Meadwell. Devn —2C 21
Meare Green. Som —1D 31
(nr. Stoke St Gregory)
Meare Green. Som —1C 31
(nr. Wrantage)
Meavy. Devn —1D 15
Meddon. Devn —2A 26
Medlyn. Corn —1B 8
Meeth. Devn —3D 27
Melbur. Corn —2B 12
Meldon. Devn —1D 21
Membury. Devn —3C 31
Menagissey. Corn —3D 11
Menerdue. Corn —1B 8
Menheniot. Corn —1A 14
Menherion. Corn —1B 8
Menna. Corn —2B 12
Merridge. Som —3C 37
Merrifield. Devn —3A 26
(nr. Bridgerule)
Merrifield. Devn —3C 17
(nr. Slapton)
Merriott. Som —2D 31
Merrivale. Devn —3D 21
Merrymeet. Corn —1A 14
Merther. Corn —3A 12
Merton. Devn —2D 27
Meshaw. Devn —2B 28
Metcombe. Devn —1A 24
Metherell. Corn —1C 15
Mevagissey. Corn —3C 13
Michaelstow. Corn —3C 19
Michelcombe. Devn —1A 16
Middle Burnham. Som —1D 37
Middlecott. Devn —2B 22
Middlehill. Corn —1A 14
Middle Marwood. Devn —3D 33
Middlemoor. Devn —3C 21
Middle Rocombe. Devn —1D 17
Middle Stoughton. Som —2D 37
Middle Taphouse. Corn —1D 13
Middle Town. IOS —1B 66
Middlewood. Corn —3A 20
Middlezoy. Som —3D 37
Mid Lambrook. Som —2D 31
Mile End. Devn —3C 23
Milford. Devn —1A 26
Millbrook. Corn —2C 15
Millbrook. Devn —3B 34
Millcombe. Corn —3B 20
Millcombe. Devn —3C 17
Millhayes. Devn —2B 30
(nr. Hemyock)
Millhayes. Devn —3C 31
(nr. Stockland)
Millhill. Devn —3C 21
Millook. Corn —1D 19
Millpool. Corn —3D 19
Milltown. Devn —3D 33
Milton. N Som —1D 37
Milton Abbot. Devn —3C 21
Milton Combe. Devn —1C 15
Milton Damerel. Devn —2B 26
Milverton. Som —1B 30
Minehead. Som —2D 35
Mingoose. Corn —3D 11
Minions. Corn —3A 20
Misterton. Som —3D 31
Mitchell. Corn —2A 12
Mithian. Corn —2D 11
Mixtow. Corn —2D 13
Modbury. Devn —2A 16
Mogworthy. Devn —2C 29
Molland. Devn —1C 29
Monkleigh. Devn —1C 27
Monkokehampton. Devn —3D 27
Monksilver. Som —3A 36
Monkton. Devn —3B 30
Monkton Heathfield. Som —1C 31
Monkton Wyld. Dors —1D 25
Moorbath. Dors —1D 25
Moorhayes. Devn —2D 29
Moorland. Som —3D 37
Moorlinch. Som —3D 37
Moorshop. Devn —3D 21
Moorswater. Corn —1A 14
Moortown. Devn —3D 21
Morchard Bishop. Devn —3B 28
Morchard Road. Devn —3B 28
Morcombelake. Dors —1D 25
Morebath. Devn —1D 29
Moreleigh. Devn —2B 16
Moretonhampstead. Devn —2B 22
Mornacott. Devn —1B 28
Mornick. Corn —3B 20
Mortehoe. Devn —2C 33
Morvah. Corn —2B 6
Morval. Corn —2A 14
Morwenstow. Corn —2A 26
Mosterton. Dors —3D 31
Mothecombe. Devn —3A 16
Mount. Corn —1D 13
Mount Ambrose. Corn —3D 11
Mount Hawke. Corn —3D 11
Mountjoy. Corn —1A 12
Mount Pleasant. Corn —1C 13
Mousehole. Corn —3B 6
Muchelney. Som —1D 31
Muchelney Ham. Som —1D 31
Muchlarnick. Corn —2A 14
Muddiford. Devn —3D 33
Muddlebridge. Devn —3D 33
Mudgley. Som —2D 37
Mullacott. Devn —2D 33
Mullacott Cross. Devn —2D 33
Mullion. Corn —3A 8
Mullion Cove. Corn —3A 8
Murchington. Devn —2A 22
Musbury. Devn —1C 25
Mutterton. Devn —3A 30
Mylor Bridge. Corn —1C 9
Mylor Churchtown. Corn —1C 9

Nailsbourne. Som —1C 31
Nancledra. Corn —2B 6
Nanpean. Corn —2B 12
Nanstallon. Corn —1C 13
Nantithet. Corn —3D 7
Narcegollan. Corn —2D 7
Narkurs. Corn —2B 14
Natcott. Devn —1A 26
Navarino. Corn —2A 20
Neopardy. Devn —1B 22
Nethercott. Devn —1B 20
Nether Exe. Devn —3D 29
Nether Stowey. Som —3B 36
Netherton. Corn —3A 20
Netherton. Devn —3C 23
Netton. Devn —3D 15
Newbridge. Corn —1B 14
(nr. Callington)
Newbridge. Corn —2B 6
(nr. Madron)
Newbridge. Corn —3D 11
(nr. Truro)
New Buildings. Devn —3B 28
Newbury. Devn —1B 22
Newcott. Devn —3C 31
Newford. IOS —1B 66
New Grimsby. IOS —1A 66
New Inn. Devn —3C 27
Newland. Som —3C 35
New Mill. Corn —2B 6
(nr. Penzance)
New Mill. Corn —3A 12
(nr. Truro)
New Mills. Corn —2A 12
New Polzeath. Corn —3B 18
Newport. Corn —2B 20
Newport. Devn —3D 33
Newport. Som —1D 31
Newquay. Corn —1A 12
Newton. Som —3B 36
Newton Abbot. Devn —3C 23
Newton Ferrers. Devn —3D 15
Newton Poppleford. Devn —2A 24
Newton St Cyres. Devn —1C 23
Newton St Petrock. Devn —2C 27
Newton Tracey. Devn —1D 27
Newtown. Corn —3A 20
New Town. Devn —1B 28
(nr. Bishop's Nympton)
Newtown. Devn —1A 24
(nr. Whimple)
Newtown. Som —2C 31
Newtown-in-St Martin. Corn —2B 8
Nicholashayne. Devn —2B 30
Nightcott. Som —1C 29
Nine Oaks. Devn —1A 24
Ninnis. Corn —3D 11
Norman's Green. Devn —3A 30
Normansland. Devn —2C 29
Norris Green. Corn —1C 15
Northam. Devn —1C 27
Northay. Som —2C 31
North Bovey. Devn —2B 22
North Brentor. Devn —2C 21
North Buckland. Devn —2C 33
North Chideock. Dors —1D 25
North Coombe. Devn —2C 29
Northcott. Devn —1B 20
(nr. Boyton)
Northcott. Devn —2A 30
(nr. Culmstock)
North Country. Corn —1D 7
North Curry. Som —1D 31
North Darley. Corn —3A 20
North End. Som —1C 31
Northfield. Som —3C 37
North Healand. Devn —2D 27
North Heasley. Devn —3B 34
North Hill. Corn —3A 20
North Huish. Devn —2B 16
Northleigh. Devn —3A 34
(nr. Barnstaple)
Northleigh. Devn —1B 24
(nr. Wilmington)
Northlew. Devn —1D 21
North Molton. Devn —1B 28
Northmoor Green. Som —3D 37
Northmostown. Devn —2A 24
North Newton. Som —3C 37
North Petherton. Som —3C 37
North Petherwin. Corn —2A 20
North Radworthy. Devn —3B 34
North Star. Devn —2A 24
North Tamerton. Corn —1B 20
North Tawton. Devn —3A 28
North Town. Devn —3D 27
Northward. IOS —1A 66
Northway. Som —1B 30
North Whilborough. Devn —1C 17
Northwick. Som —2D 37
Norton. Devn —2C 17
(nr. Dartmouth)
Norton. Devn —1A 26
(nr. Hartland)
Norton Fitzwarren. Som —1B 30
Noss Mayo. Devn —3D 15

70 Visitors' Devon & Cornwall Atlas

Notter—Shipham

Notter. *Corn* —1B **14**
Nymet Rowland. *Devn* —3B **28**
Nymet Tracey. *Devn* —3B **28**
Nynehead. *Som* —1B **30**

Oak Cross. *Devn* —1D **21**
Oake. *Som* —1B **30**
Oakford. *Devn* —1D **29**
Oakfordbridge. *Devn* —1D **29**
Oare. *Som* —2C **35**
Oareford. *Som* —2C **35**
Oath. *Som* —1D **31**
Offwell. *Devn* —1B **24**
Okehampton. *Devn* —1D **21**
Oldborough. *Devn* —3B **28**
Old Cleeve. *Som* —2A **36**
Old Grimsby. *IOS* —1A **66**
Old Kea. *Corn* —3A **12**
Old Mill. *Corn* —3B **20**
Oldmixon. *N Som* —1D **37**
Oldridge. *Devn* —1C **23**
Old Town. *IOS* —1B **66**
Oldways End. *Devn* —1C **29**
Orchard Hill. *Devn* —1C **27**
Orchard Portman. *Som* —1C **31**
Oreston. *Plym* —2D **15**
Othery. *Som* —3D **37**
Otterham. *Corn* —1D **19**
Otterhampton. *Som* —2C **37**
Otterton. *Devn* —2A **24**
Ottery St Mary. *Devn* —1B **24**
Outer Hope. *Devn* —3A **16**
Over Stowey. *Som* —3B **36**
Over Stratton. *Som* —2D **31**
Oxenpill. *Som* —2D **37**

Padson. *Devn* —1D **21**
Padstow. *Corn* —3B **18**
Paignton. *Devn* —1C **17**
Pancrasweek. *Devn* —3A **26**
Pantersbridge. *Corn* —1D **13**
Par. *Corn* —2C **13**
Paramoor. *Corn* —3B **12**
Park Bottom. *Corn* —1D **7**
Parkfield. *Corn* —1B **14**
Parkham. *Devn* —1B **26**
Parkham Ash. *Devn* —1B **26**
Parracombe. *Devn* —2A **34**
Patchacott. *Devn* —1C **21**
Patchole. *Devn* —2A **34**
Pathe. *Som* —3D **37**
Paul. *Corn* —3B **6**
Pawlett. *Som* —2C **37**
Payhembury. *Devn* —3A **30**
Paynter's Cross. *Corn* —1B **14**
Paynter's Lane End. *Corn* —1D **7**
Payton. *Som* —1B **30**
Pedwell. *Som* —3D **37**
Pelynt. *Corn* —2A **14**
Penare. *Corn* —3C **13**
Penbeagle. *Corn* —2C **7**
Penberth. *Corn* —3B **6**
Pencalenick. *Corn* —3A **12**
Pencarrow. *Corn* —2D **19**
Pencoys. *Corn* —2D **7**
Pendeen. *Corn* —2A **6**
Pendoggett. *Corn* —3C **19**
Peneleway. *Corn* —3A **12**
Pengersick. *Corn* —3C **7**
Penhale. *Corn* —2B **12** (nr. Fraddon)
Penhale. *Corn* —2C **15** (nr. Millbrook)
Penhale. *Corn* —3A **8** (nr. Mullion)
Penhale Camp. *Corn* —2D **11**
Penhallick. *Corn* —1D **7**
Penhallow. *Corn* —2D **11**
Penhalvean. *Corn* —1B **8**
Penjerrick. *Corn* —1B **8**
Penmarth. *Corn* —1B **8**
Penmayne. *Corn* —3B **18**
Pennance. *Corn* —3D **11**
Pennycross. *Plym* —2C **15**
Pennymoor. *Devn* —2C **29**
Penpethy. *Corn* —2C **19**
Penpillick. *Corn* —2C **13**
Penpol. *Corn* —1C **9**
Penpoll. *Corn* —2D **13**
Penponds. *Corn* —2D **7**
Penpont. *Corn* —3C **19**
Penquit. *Devn* —2A **16**
Penrose. *Corn* —3A **18**
Penrose Hill. *Corn* —3D **7**
Penryn. *Corn* —1B **8**
Pensilva. *Corn* —1A **14**
Penstone. *Devn* —3B **28**
Pentewan. *Corn* —3C **13**
Pentire. *Corn* —1D **11**
Pentireglaze. *Corn* —3B **18**
Penvose. *Corn* —3B **12**
Penwartha. *Corn* —2D **11**
Penwithick. *Corn* —2C **13**
Penzance. *Corn* —2B **6**
Percull. *Corn* —1C **9**
Periton. *Som* —2D **35**
Perranarworthal. *Corn* —1B **8**
Perrancoombe. *Corn* —2D **11**
Perranporth. *Corn* —2D **11**
Perranuthnoe. *Corn* —3C **7**
Perranwell. *Corn* —1B **8** (nr. Perranarworthal)
Perranwell. *Corn* —2D **11** (nr. Perranporth)
Perran Wharf. *Corn* —1B **8**
Perranzabuloe. *Corn* —2D **11**
Perry Green. *Som* —3C **37**
Perry Street. *Som* —3D **31**
Peter's Marland. *Devn* —2C **27**
Peter Tavy. *Devn* —3D **21**
Petherwin Gate. *Corn* —2A **20**
Petrockstowe. *Devn* —3D **27**
Petton. *Devn* —1A **30**
Philham. *Devn* —1A **26**
Phillack. *Corn* —2C **7**
Philleigh. *Corn* —1C **9**
Pibsbury. *Som* —1D **31**
Pickney. *Som* —1B **30**
Pickwell. *Devn* —2C **33**
Piece. *Corn* —2D **7**
Pightley. *Som* —3C **37**
Pillaton. *Corn* —1B **14**
Pillatonmill. *Corn* —1B **14**
Pilsdon. *Dors* —1D **25**
Pinhoe. *Devn* —1D **23**
Pipers Pool. *Corn* —2A **20**
Pippacott. *Devn* —3D **33**
Pirzwell. *Devn* —3A **30**
Pitminster. *Som* —2C **31**
Pitney. *Som* —1D **31**
Pitsford Hill. *Som* —3A **36**
Pitt. *Devn* —2A **30**
Pityme. *Corn* —3B **18**
Plainsfield. *Som* —3B **36**
Playing Place. *Corn* —3A **12**
Plusha. *Corn* —2A **20**
Plushabridge. *Corn* —3B **20**
Plymouth. *Plym* —2C **15**
Plympton. *Plym* —2D **15**
Plymstock. *Plym* —2D **15**
Plymtree. *Devn* —3A **30**
Polbathic. *Corn* —2B **14**
Polbrock. *Corn* —1C **13**
Polgigga. *Corn* —3A **6**
Polgooth. *Corn* —2B **12**
Polgrain. *Corn* —3B **12**
Polladras. *Corn* —2D **7**
Polmarth. *Corn* —1B **8**
Polmassick. *Corn* —3B **12**
Polmear. *Corn* —2C **13**
Polperro. *Corn* —2A **14**
Polruan. *Corn* —2D **13**
Polscoe. *Corn* —1D **13**
Polstreath. *Corn* —3C **13**
Poltesco. *Corn* —3B **8**
Poltimore. *Devn* —1D **23**
Polyphant. *Corn* —2A **20**
Polzeath. *Corn* —3B **18**
Ponsanooth. *Corn* —1B **8**
Ponsongath. *Corn* —3B **8**
Ponsworthy. *Devn* —3B **22**
Pont. *Corn* —2D **13**
Pool. *Corn* —1D **7**
Popham. *Devn* —3B **34**
Porkellis. *Corn* —2D **7**
Porlock. *Som* —2C **35**
Porlock Weir. *Som* —2C **35**
Portcothan. *Corn* —3A **18**
Port Eliot. *Corn* —2B **14**
Portgate. *Devn* —2C **21**
Portgaverne. *Corn* —2C **19**
Porth. *Corn* —1A **12**
Porthallow. *Corn* —2A **14**
Porthcurno. *Corn* —3A **6**
Porthgwarra. *Corn* —3A **6**
Porthhallow. *Corn* —2B **8**
Porth Kea. *Corn* —3A **12**
Porthleven. *Corn* —3D **7**
Porthloo. *IOS* —1B **66**
Porthmeor. *Corn* —2B **6**
Porth Navas. *Corn* —2B **8**
Portholland. *Corn* —3B **12**
Porthoustock. *Corn* —2C **9**
Porthtowan. *Corn* —1D **7**
Portington. *Devn* —3C **21**
Port Isaac. *Corn* —2B **18**
Portloe. *Corn* —1D **9**
Portlooe. *Corn* —2A **14**
Portmellon. *Corn* —3C **13**
Portquin. *Corn* —2B **18**
Portreath. *Corn* —1D **7**
Portscatho. *Corn* —1C **9**
Portwrinkle. *Corn* —2B **14**
Postbridge. *Devn* —3A **22**
Pottington. *Devn* —3D **33**
Poughill. *Corn* —3A **26**
Poughill. *Devn* —3C **29**
Poundsgate. *Devn* —3B **22**
Poundstock. *Corn* —1A **20**
Powderham. *Devn* —2D **23**
Praa Sands. *Corn* —3C **7**
Praze-an-Beeble. *Corn* —2D **7**
Prescott. *Devn* —2A **30**
Preston. *Devn* —3C **23**
Preston Bowyer. *Som* —1B **30**
Princetown. *Devn* —3D **21**
Prixford. *Devn* —3D **33**
Probus. *Corn* —3A **12**
Prospidnick. *Corn* —2D **7**
Prussia Cove. *Corn* —3C **7**
Puckington. *Som* —2D **31**
Puddington Bottom. *Devn* —2C **29**
Puriton. *Som* —2D **37**
Purtington. *Som* —3D **31**
Putsborough. *Devn* —2C **33**
Puxton. *N Som* —1D **37**
Pyleigh. *Som* —3B **36**
Pyworthy. *Devn* —3B **26**

Queen Dart. *Devn* —2C **29**
Quethlock. *Corn* —1B **14**
Quintrell Downs. *Corn* —1A **12**

Rackenford. *Devn* —2C **29**
Raleigh Hill. *Devn* —1C **27**
Rame. *Corn* —3C **15** (nr. Millbrook)
Rame. *Corn* —1B **8** (nr. Penryn)
Ramsley. *Devn* —1A **22**
Rapps. *Som* —2D **31**
Rattery. *Devn* —1B **16**
Ravenshayes. *Devn* —3D **29**
Rawridge. *Devn* —3C **31**
Raymond's Hill. *Devn* —1D **25**
Reawla. *Corn* —2D **7**
Redgate. *Corn* —1A **14**
Redmoor. *Corn* —1C **13**
Red Post. *Corn* —3A **26**
Redruth. *Corn* —3D **11**
Reedy. *Devn* —2C **23**
Rejerrah. *Corn* —2A **12**
Releath. *Corn* —2D **7**
Relubbus. *Corn* —2C **7**
Rescassa. *Corn* —3B **12**
Rescoria. *Corn* —3B **12**
Rescorla. *Corn* —2C **13**
Reskadinnick. *Corn* —1D **7**
Resugga Green. *Corn* —2C **13**
Retallack. *Corn* —1B **12**
Retire. *Corn* —1C **13**
Rewe. *Devn* —1D **23**
Rexon. *Devn* —2C **21**
Rezare. *Corn* —3B **20**
Rhode. *Som* —3C **37**
Riddlecombe. *Devn* —2A **28**
Rilla Mill. *Corn* —3A **20**
Rimpston. *Devn* —3B **16**
Ringmore. *Devn* —3A **16** (nr. Challaborough)
Ringmore. *Devn* —3D **23** (nr. Teignmouth)
Rinsey. *Corn* —3C **7**
Rinsey Croft. *Corn* —3D **7**
Rising Sun. *Corn* —3B **20**
Riverton. *Devn* —3A **34**
Roachill. *Devn* —1C **29**
Road Green. *Devn* —1C **25**
Roadwater. *Som* —3A **36**
Roborough. *Devn* —2D **27** (nr. Great Torrington)
Roborough. *Devn* —1D **15** (nr. Plymouth)
Roche. *Corn* —1B **12**
Rock. *Corn* —3B **18**
Rockbeare. *Devn* —1A **24**
Rockford. *Devn* —2B **34**
Rockwell Green. *Som* —1B **30**
Rodhuish. *Som* —3A **36**
Rodway. *Som* —2C **37**
Romansleigh. *Devn* —1B **28**
Rooks Bridge. *Som* —1D **37**
Rook's Nest. *Som* —3A **36**
Roscroggan. *Corn* —1D **7**
Rose. *Corn* —2D **11**
Rose Ash. *Devn* —1B **28**
Rosecare. *Corn* —1D **19**
Rosedinnick. *Corn* —1B **12**
Rosedown. *Devn* —1A **26**
Rosemary Lane. *Devn* —2B **30**
Rosemergy. *Corn* —2B **6**
Rosenannon. *Corn* —1B **12**
Rosevean. *Corn* —2C **13**
Rosevine. *Corn* —1C **9**
Rosewarne. *Corn* —2D **7**
Roseworthy. *Corn* —2D **7** (nr. Camborne)
Roseworthy. *Corn* —3D **11** (nr. Truro)
Roskorwell. *Corn* —2B **8**
Rosudgeon. *Corn* —3C **7**
Roundham. *Som* —3D **31**
Rousdon. *Devn* —1C **25**
Row. *Corn* —3C **19**
Rowberrow. *Som* —1D **37**
Rowden. *Devn* —1A **22**
Royston Water. *Som* —2C **31**
Ruan High Lanes. *Corn* —1D **9**
Ruan Lanihorne. *Corn* —3A **12**
Ruan Major. *Corn* —3B **8**
Ruan Minor. *Corn* —3B **8**
Ruddlemoor. *Corn* —2C **13**
Rulshton. *Som* —1C **31**
Rumford. *Corn* —3A **18**
Rumsam. *Devn* —3D **33**
Rumwell. *Som* —1B **30**
Rundlestone. *Devn* —3D **21**
Runnington. *Som* —1B **30**
Rushford. *Devn* —3C **21**
Ruthernbridge. *Corn* —1C **13**
Ruthvoes. *Corn* —1B **12**
Ryall. *Dors* —1D **25**

St Agnes. *Corn* —2D **11**
St Allen. *Corn* —2A **12**
St Ann's Chapel. *Corn* —3C **21**
St Ann's Chapel. *Devn* —3A **16**
St Anthony. *Corn* —1C **9**
St Anthony-in-Meneage. *Corn* —2B **8**
St Austell. *Corn* —2C **13**
St Blazey. *Corn* —2C **13**
St Blazey Gate. *Corn* —2C **13**
St Breock. *Corn* —3B **18**
St Breward. *Corn* —3C **19**
St Budeaux. *Plym* —2C **15**
St Buryan. *Corn* —3B **6**
St Cleer. *Corn* —1A **14**
St Clement. *Corn* —3A **12**
St Clether. *Corn* —2A **20**
St Columb Major. *Corn* —1B **12**
St Columb Minor. *Corn* —1A **12**
St Columb Road. *Corn* —2B **12**
St Day. *Corn* —3D **11**
St Dennis. *Corn* —2B **12**
St Dominick. *Corn* —1B **14**
St Dympna's. *Devn* —1C **25**
St Endellion. *Corn* —3B **18**
St Enoder. *Corn* —2A **12**
St Erme. *Corn* —3A **12**
St Erney. *Corn* —2B **14**
St Erth. *Corn* —2C **7**
St Erth Praze. *Corn* —2C **7**
St Ervan. *Corn* —3A **18**
St Eval. *Corn* —1A **12**
St Ewe. *Corn* —3B **12**
St Gennys. *Corn* —1D **19**
St Georges. *N Som* —1D **37**
St Germans. *Corn* —2B **14**
St Giles in the Wood. *Devn* —2D **27**
St Giles on the Heath. *Devn* —1B **20**
St Gluvias. *Corn* —1B **8**
St Hilary. *Corn* —2C **7**
Saint Hill. *Devn* —3A **30**
St Issey. *Corn* —3B **18**
St Ive. *Corn* —1B **14**
St Ives. *Corn* —1C **7**
St Jidgey. *Corn* —1B **12**
St John. *Corn* —2C **15**
St John's Chapel. *Devn* —1D **27**
St Just. *Corn* —2A **6**
St Just in Roseland. *Corn* —1C **9**
St Keverne. *Corn* —2B **8**
St Kew. *Corn* —3C **19**
St Kew Highway. *Corn* —3C **19**
St Keyne. *Corn* —1A **14**
St Lawrence. *Corn* —1C **13**
St Levan. *Corn* —3A **6**
St Loy. *Corn* —3B **6**
St Mabyn. *Corn* —3C **19**
St Martin. *Corn* —2B **8** (nr. Helston)
St Martin. *Corn* —2A **14** (nr. Looe)
St Mawes. *Corn* —1C **9**
St Mawgan. *Corn* —1A **12**
St Mellon. *Corn* —1B **14**
St Merryn. *Corn* —3A **18**
St Mewan. *Corn* —2B **12**
St Michael Caerhays. *Corn* —3B **12**
St Michael Penkevil. *Corn* —3A **12**
St Minver. *Corn* —3B **18**
St Neot. *Corn* —1D **13**
St Newlyn East. *Corn* —2A **12**
St Ruan. *Corn* —3B **8**
St Stephen. *Corn* —2B **12**
St Stephens. *Corn* —2B **20** (nr. Launceston)
St Stephens. *Corn* —2C **15** (nr. Saltash)
St Teath. *Corn* —2C **19**
St Thomas. *Devn* —1D **23**
St Tudy. *Corn* —3C **19**
St Veep. *Corn* —2D **13**
St Wenn. *Corn* —1B **12**
St Winnolls. *Corn* —2B **14**
St Winnow. *Corn* —2D **13**
Salcombe Regis. *Devn* —2B **24**
Saltash. *Corn* —2C **15**
Saltrens. *Devn* —1C **27**
Salwayash. *Dors* —1D **25**
Samford Arundel. *Som* —2B **30**
Samford Moor. *Som* —2B **30**
Samford Peverell. *Devn* —2A **30**
Sampford Brett. *Som* —2A **36**
Sampford Chapple. *Devn* —3A **28**
Sampford Courtenay. *Devn* —3A **28**
Sampford Spiney. *Devn* —3D **21**
Sancreed. *Corn* —3B **6**
Sand. *Som* —2D **37**
Sandford. *Devn* —3C **29**
Sandford. *N Som* —1D **37**
Sandplace. *Corn* —2A **14**
Sandy Park. *Devn* —2B **22**
Satterleigh. *Devn* —1A **28**
Saunton. *Devn* —3C **33**
Scarcewater. *Corn* —2B **12**
Scobbiscombe. *Devn* —3A **16**
Scorrier. *Corn* —3D **11**
Scorriton. *Devn* —1B **16**
Sea. *Som* —2D **31**
Seaborough. *Dors* —3D **31**
Seaton. *Corn* —2B **14**
Seaton. *Devn* —1C **25**
Seaton Junction. *Devn* —1C **25**
Seatown. *Dors* —1D **25**
Seavington St Mary. *Som* —2D **31**
Seavington St Michael. *Som* —2D **31**
Selworthy. *Som* —2D **35**
Sennen. *Corn* —3A **6**
Sennen Cove. *Corn* —3A **6**
Seven Ash. *Som* —3B **36**
Seworgan. *Corn* —1B **8**
Shaldon. *Devn* —3D **23**
Shallowford. *Devn* —2B **34** (nr. Lynton)
Shallowford. *Devn* —3A **22** (nr. Pansworthy)
Shapwick. *Som* —3D **37**
Shaugh Prior. *Devn* —1D **15**
Shearston. *Som* —3C **37**
Shebbear. *Devn* —3C **27**
Sheepstor. *Devn* —1D **15**
Sheepwash. *Devn* —3C **27** (nr. Black Torrington)
Sheepwash. *Devn* —1B **28** (nr. Molland)
Sheffield. *Corn* —3B **6**
Sheldon. *Devn* —3B **30**
Shepherds. *Corn* —2A **12**
Shepton Beauchamp. *Som* —2D **31**
Sherford. *Devn* —3B **16**
Sherwood Green. *Devn* —1D **27**
Sheviock. *Corn* —2B **14**
Shillingford. *Devn* —1D **29**
Shillingford Abbot. *Devn* —2D **23**
Shillingford St George. *Devn* —2D **23**
Shinner's Bridge. *Devn* —1B **16**
Shipham. *Som* —1D **37**

Upton. *Corn* —3A **20**
(nr. Linkinhorne)
Upton. *Devn* —3A **30**
Upton. *Som* —1D **29**
Upton Cross. *Corn* —3A **20**
Upton Hellions. *Devn* —3C **29**
Upton Pyne. *Devn* —1D **23**
Uton. *Devn* —1C **23**

Valley Truckle. *Corn* —2D **19**
Velator. *Devn* —3C **33**
Yellow. *Som* —3A **36**
Velly. *Devn* —1A **26**
Venhay. *Devn* —2B **28**
Venn. *Devn* —3B **16**
Venngreen. *Devn* —2B **26**
Venn Ottery. *Devn* —1A **24**
Venny Tedburn. *Devn* —1C **23**
Venton. *Devn* —2D **15**
(nr. Sparkwell)
Venton. *Devn* —1A **22**
(nr. Throwleigh)
Ventongimps. *Corn* —2D **11**
Veryan. *Corn* —1D **9**
Veryan Green. *Corn* —3B **12**
Vicarage. *Devn* —2C **25**
Victoria. *Corn* —1B **12**
Virginstow. *Devn* —1B **20**
Viscar. *Corn* —1B **8**
Vole. *Som* —2D **37**

Wadderton. *Devn* —2C **17**
Waddon. *Devn* —3C **23**
Wadeford. *Som* —2D **31**
Wadland Barton. *Devn* —1D **21**
Wainhouse Corner. *Corn* —1D **19**
Walkhampton. *Devn* —1D **15**
Wall. *Corn* —2D **7**
Wambrook. *Som* —3C **31**
Wapsworthy. *Devn* —2D **21**
Warbstow. *Corn* —1A **20**
Warbstow Cross. *Corn* —1A **20**
Warkleigh. *Devn* —1A **28**
Warleggan. *Corn* —1D **13**
Washaway. *Corn* —1C **13**
Washbourne. *Devn* —2B **16**
Washfield. *Devn* —2D **29**
Washford. *Som* —2A **36**
Washford Pyne. *Devn* —2C **29**
Watchet. *Som* —2A **36**
Watchfield. *Som* —2D **37**
Water. *Devn* —2B **22**
Watergate. *Corn* —2D **19**
Watergate. *Corn* —2D **21**
Waterhead. *Devn* —3A **16**
Waterloo. *Corn* —3D **19**

Waterrow. *Som* —1A **30**
Wayford. *Som* —3D **31**
Waytown. *Devn* —1B **26**
Way Village. *Devn* —2C **29**
Weare. *Som* —1D **37**
Weare Giffard. *Devn* —1C **27**
Wearne. *Som* —1D **31**
Webberton Cross. *Devn* —2C **23**
Wedmore. *Som* —2D **37**
Week. *Devn* —1D **27**
(nr. Bishop's Tawton)
Week. *Devn* —1A **28**
(nr. North Tawton)
Week. *Devn* —2B **28**
(nr. Romansleigh)
Week. *Devn* —3D **35**
Weeke. *Devn* —1A **24**
Week Green. *Corn* —1A **20**
Week St Mary. *Corn* —1A **20**
Weir Quay. *Devn* —1C **15**
Welcombe. *Devn* —2A **26**
Wellington. *Som* —1B **30**
Welsford. *Devn* —1A **26**
Wembdon. *Som* —3C **37**
Wembury. *Devn* —3D **15**
Wembworthy. *Devn* —3A **28**
Wendron. *Corn* —2D **7**
Wenfordbridge. *Corn* —3C **19**
Werrington. *Devn* —2B **20**
West Alvington. *Devn* —3B **16**
West Anstey. *Devn* —1C **29**
West Bagborough. *Som* —3B **36**
West Buckland. *Devn* —3A **34**
West Buckland. *Som* —1B **30**
West Charleton. *Devn* —3B **16**
Westcott. *Devn* —3A **30**
West Curry. *Corn* —1A **20**
West Down. *Devn* —2D **33**
Westdowns. *Corn* —2C **19**
Westford. *Som* —1B **30**
Westham. *Som* —2D **37**
West Hatch. *Som* —1C **31**
Westhay. *Som* —2D **37**
West Hill. *Devn* —1A **24**
West Huntspill. *Som* —2D **37**
West Illkerton. *Devn* —2B **34**
West Kimber. *Devn* —1C **21**
Westlake. *Devn* —2A **16**
West Lambrook. *Som* —2D **31**
Westleigh. *Devn* —1C **27**
(nr. Bideford)
West Leigh. *Devn* —2B **16**
(nr. Harberton)
Westleigh. *Devn* —2A **30**
(nr. Holcombe Rogus)
West Leigh. *Devn* —3A **28**
(nr. Nymet Rowland)
West Looe. *Corn* —2A **14**
West Lyn. *Devn* —2B **34**

West Monkton. *Som* —1C **31**
West Newton. *Som* —1C **31**
West Ogwell. *Devn* —3C **23**
Weston. *Devn* —2B **24**
Westonzoyland. *Som* —3D **37**
Westown. *Devn* —2B **30**
West Panson. *Devn* —1B **20**
West Pentire. *Corn* —1D **11**
West Porlock. *Som* —2C **35**
Westport. *Som* —1D **31**
West Putford. *Devn* —2B **26**
West Sandford. *Devn* —3C **29**
West Stoughton. *Som* —2D **37**
West Taphouse. *Corn* —1D **13**
West Town. *Devn* —1C **23**
(nr. Exeter)
West Town. *Devn* —1B **26**
(nr. Woolfardsworthy)
Westward Ho!. *Devn* —1C **27**
West Wembury. *Devn* —3D **15**
West Wick. *N Som* —1D **37**
Westwood. *Devn* —1A **24**
West Worlington. *Devn* —2B **28**
West Youlstone. *Corn* —2A **26**
Weycroft. *Devn* —1D **25**
Whatley. *Som* —3D **31**
Wheal Baddon. *Corn* —3D **11**
Wheal Frances. *Corn* —2D **11**
Wheal Rose. *Corn* —3D **11**
Wheatley. *Devn* —1C **23**
Wheddon Cross. *Som* —3D **35**
Whiddon Down. *Devn* —1A **22**
Whimble. *Devn* —3B **26**
Whimple. *Devn* —1A **24**
Whipcott. *Devn* —2A **30**
Whipton. *Devn* —1D **23**
Whitchurch. *Devn* —3C **21**
Whitchurch Canonicorum.
                    Dors —1D **25**
White Cross. *Corn* —3D **7**
(nr. Mullion)
White Cross. *Corn* —2A **12**
(nr. St Columb Road)
Whitecross. *Corn* —3B **18**
(nr. Wadebridge)
White Cross. *Devn* —1A **24**
Whitefield. *Som* —1A **30**
Whitehall. *Devn* —3D **33**
(nr. Barnstaple)
Whitehall. *Devn* —2B **30**
(nr. Hemyock)
Whitelackington. *Som* —2D **31**
Whitemoor. *Corn* —2B **12**
Whitestaunton. *Som* —2C **31**
Whitestone. *Devn* —1C **23**
Whiteworks. *Devn* —3A **22**
Whitford. *Devn* —1C **25**
Whitleigh. *Plym* —1C **15**
Whitnage. *Devn* —2A **30**

Whitstone. *Corn* —1A **20**
Wick. *Devn* —3B **30**
Wick. *Som* —1D **37**
(nr. East Brent)
Wick. *Som* —2C **37**
(nr. Stogursey)
Widecombe in the Moor.
                    Devn —3B **22**
Widegates. *Corn* —2A **14**
Widemouth Bay. *Corn* —3A **26**
Widmouth. *Devn* —2D **33**
Widworthy. *Devn* —1C **25**
Wiggaton. *Devn* —1B **24**
Wiland. *Som* —2B **30**
Wilcove. *Corn* —2C **15**
Willand. *Devn* —2A **30**
Willet. *Som* —3B **36**
Willingcott. *Devn* —2C **33**
Willsworthy. *Devn* —2D **21**
Wilmington. *Devn* —1C **25**
Wilminstone. *Devn* —3C **21**
Wilsham. *Devn* —2B **34**
Wiltown. *Devn* —2B **30**
Windmill. *Corn* —3A **18**
Windmill Hill. *Som* —2D **31**
Winkleigh. *Devn* —3A **28**
Winnard's Perch. *Corn* —1B **12**
Winscombe. *N Som* —1D **37**
Winsford. *Som* —3D **35**
Winsham. *Devn* —3C **33**
Winsham. *Som* —3D **31**
Winswell. *Devn* —2C **27**
Withacott. *Devn* —2C **27**
Witheridge. *Devn* —2C **29**
Withiel. *Corn* —1B **12**
Withiel Florey. *Som* —3D **35**
Withielgoose Mills. *Corn* —1C **13**
Withleigh. *Devn* —2D **29**
Withycombe. *Som* —2A **36**
Withycombe Raleigh. *Devn*
                    —2A **24**
Withypool. *Som* —3C **35**
Wiveliscombe. *Som* —1A **30**
Wonson. *Devn* —2A **22**
Woodacott. *Devn* —3B **26**
Woodacott Cross. *Devn* —3B **26**
Woodbrooke. *Devn* —1B **22**
Woodbury. *Devn* —2A **24**
Woodbury Salterton. *Devn*
                    —2A **24**
Woodcombe. *Som* —2D **35**
Woodfoed. *Devn* —1B **24**
Woodford. *Corn* —2A **26**
Woodford. *Devn* —2B **16**
Woodford. *Plym* —2D **15**
Woodgate. *Devn* —2B **30**
Woodland. *Devn* —1B **16**
Woodland Head. *Devn* —1B **22**
Woodleigh. *Devn* —3B **16**

Woodmanton. *Devn* —2A **24**
Woodsdown Hill. *Devn* —3B **26**
Woodtown. *Devn* —1C **27**
(nr. Bideford)
Woodtown. *Devn* —1C **27**
(nr. Saltrens)
Woody Bay. *Devn* —2A **34**
Woolacombe. *Devn* —2C **33**
Woolavington. *Som* —2D **37**
Woolcotts. *Som* —3D **35**
Wooley. *Corn* —2A **26**
Woolfardisworthy. *Devn* —3C **29**
(nr. Crediton)
Woolfardisworthy. *Devn* —1B **26**
(nr. Parkham)
Woollaton. *Devn* —2C **27**
Woolmersdon. *Som* —3C **37**
Woolminstone. *Som* —3D **31**
Woolsery. *Devn* —1B **26**
Woolsgrove. *Devn* —3B **28**
Woolston. *Corn* —1A **14**
Woolston. *Devn* —3B **16**
Woolston. *Som* —3A **36**
Woolston Green. *Devn* —1B **16**
Woolwell. *Devn* —1D **15**
Wootton Courtenay. *Som*
                    —2D **35**
Wootton Fitzpaine. *Dors* —1D **25**
Worle. *N Som* —1D **37**
Worlington. *Devn* —3C **33**
Wotter. *Devn* —1D **15**
Wrafton. *Devn* —3C **33**
Wrangway. *Som* —2B **30**
Wrantage. *Som* —1D **31**
Wrayland. *Devn* —2B **22**
Wressing. *Devn* —3A **30**
Wringworthy. *Corn* —2A **14**

Yalberton. *Devn* —2C **17**
Yarcombe. *Devn* —3C **31**
Yarde. *Som* —3A **36**
Yarnscombe. *Devn* —1D **27**
Yarrow. *Som* —2D **37**
Yate. *Devn* —3D **29**
Yealmpton. *Devn* —2D **15**
Yelland. *Devn* —3C **33**
Yelverton. *Devn* —1D **15**
Yeoford. *Devn* —1B **22**
Yeolmbridge. *Corn* —2B **20**
Yeo Mill. *Devn* —1C **29**
Yettington. *Devn* —2A **24**
Yondertown. *Devn* —2D **15**

Zeal Monachorum. *Devn*
                    —3B **28**
Zelah. *Corn* —2A **12**
Zennor. *Corn* —2B **6**

HOW TO USE THE PLACES OF INTEREST INDEX

Places of interest are represented by the appropriate symbol on the map together with red text in a yellow box. The index reference is to the square in which the symbol (or its pointer) appears, not to the text box; e.g. Bampton —1D **29** is to be found in square 1D on page **29**. The page number being shown in bold type.

Entries shown without an index reference have the name of the appropriate town plan on which they appear. For reasons of clarity, these places of interest do not appear on the main map pages. The extent of these town plans are indicated on the main pages by a blue box.

Terms such as 'museum', 'country park' etc. are omitted from the text on the map.

Entries in italics are not named on the map but are shown with a symbol.
Entries in italics and enclosed in brackets are not shown on the map.
For both these types of entry, the nearest village or town name is given, where that name is not already included in the name of the place of interest.

Opening times for places of interest vary considerably depending on the season, day of week or the ownership of the property. Please check with the nearest tourist information centre listed below before starting your journey.

Tourist Information Centre (Open All Year)

Bampton — 1D **29**
Barnstaple, Tel: 01271 375000
Bideford — 1C **27**, Tel: 01237 477676 / 421853
Bodmin, Tel: 01208 76616
Boscastle — 1D **19**, Tel: 01840 250010
Braunton — 3C **33**, Tel: 01271 816400
Bridgwater — 3C **37**, Tel: 01278 427652
Brixham, Tel: 01803 852861
Bude, Tel: 01288 354240
Budleigh Salterton — 2A **24**, Tel: 01395 445275
Burnham-on-Sea — 2D **37**, Tel: 01278 787852
Chard — 3D **31**, Tel: 01460 67463
Dartmouth, Tel: 01803 834224
Dawlish — 3D **23**, Tel: 01626 863589
Exeter Services, M5, junction 30 — 1D **23**,
  Tel: 01392 437581
Exeter, Tel: 01392 265700
Exmouth — 2A **24**, Tel: 01395 222299
Falmouth, Tel: 01326 312300
Fowey, Tel: 01726 833616
Great Torrington — 2C **27**, Tel: 01805 623302
Helston & Lizard Peninsula — 3D **7**,
  Tel: 01326 565431
Holsworthy — 3B **26**, Tel: 01409 254185
Honiton — 3B **30**, Tel: 01404 43716
Ilfracombe, Tel: 01271 863001
Isles of Scilly, Hugh Town, St Mary's, Isles of Scilly
  — 1B **66**, Tel: 01720 422536
Ivybridge — 2A **16**, Tel: 01752 897035
Kingsbridge — 3B **16**, Tel: 01548 853195
Launceston — 1C **19**, Tel: 01566 772321 / 772333
Lostwithiel — 2D **13**, Tel: 01208 872207
Lyme Regis — 1D **25**, Tel: 01297 442138
Lynton, Tel: 01598 752225
Mevagissey — 3C **13**, Tel: 01726 842266
Minehead, Tel: 01643 702624
Newquay, Tel: 01637 871345
Newton Abbot, Tel: 01626 367494
Padstow, Tel: 01841 533449
Paignton, Tel: 01803 558383
Penzance, Tel: 01736 362207
Perranporth — 2D **11**, Tel: 01872 573368
Plymouth Discovery Centre, Crabtree, Plymouth
  — 2D **15**, Tel: 01752 266030 / 266031
Plymouth, Tel: 01752 304849
St Ives, Tel: 01736 796297
Salcombe — 3B **16**, Tel: 01548 843927
Seaton — 2C **25**, Tel: 01297 21660 / 21689
Sidmouth — 2B **24**, Tel: 01395 516441
Somerset Visitor Centre, M5 (Southbound),
  East Brent — 1D **37**, Tel: 01934 750833
Taunton, Tel: 01823 336344
Tavistock — 3C **21**, Tel: 01822 612938
Teignmouth — 3D **23**, Tel: 01626 779769
Tiverton — 2D **29**, Tel: 01884 255827
Torquay, Tel: 01803 297428
Totnes — 1C **17**, Tel: 01803 863168
Truro, Tel: 01872 274555
Wadebridge — 3B **18**, Tel: 01208 813725
Wellington — 1B **30**, Tel: 01823 663379
Weston-super-Mare — 1D **37**, Tel: 01934 888800

Tourist Information Centre (Summer Season Only)

Ashburton Community Information Point
  — 1B **16**, Tel: 01364 653426

Axminster — 1C **25**, Tel: 01297 34386
Bovey Tracey — 3C **23**, Tel: 01626 832047
Camelford — 2D **19**, Tel: 01840 212954
Combe Martin — 2D **33**, Tel: 01271 883319
Crediton — 3C **29**, Tel: 01363 772006
Crewkerne — 3D **31**, Tel: 01460 73441
Hayle — 2C **7**, Tel: 01736 754399
Ilminster — 2D **31**, Tel: 01460 57294
Langport — 1D **31**, Tel: 01458 253527
Looe, Tel: 01503 262072
Modbury — 2A **16**, Tel: 01548 830159
Okehampton — 1D **21**, Tel: 01837 53020
Ottery St Mary — 1A **24**, Tel: 01404 813964
Polzeath — 3B **18**, Tel: 01208 862488
Porlock — 2C **35**, Tel: 01643 863150
St Austell — 2C **13**, Tel: 01726 76333
Shaldon Tourist Centre — 3D **23**,
  Tel: 01626 873723
South Molton — 1B **28**, Tel: 01769 574122
Tiverton Services, M5, junction 27 — 2A **30**,
  Tel: 01884 821242
Watchet Tourism Office — 2A **36**
Woolacombe — 2C **33**, Tel: 01271 870553

Visitor Centre/Information Centre (National Park)

Combe Martin Visitor Centre NP — 2D **33**,
  Tel: 01271 883319
County Gate Visitor Centre NP — 2B **34**,
  Tel: 01598 741321
Dulverton Visitor Centre NP — 1D **29**,
  Tel: 01398 323841
Dunster Visitor Centre NP — 2D **35**,
  Tel: 01643 821835
Haytor Information Centre, Haytor Vale NP
  — 3B **22**, Tel: 01364 661520
High Moorland Visitor Centre, Princetown NP
  — 3D **21**, Tel: 01822 890414
Lynmouth Visitor Centre NP — Lynton & Lynmouth,
  Tel: 01598 752509
Moretonhampstead Visitor Information Centre NP
  — 2B **22**, Tel: 01647 440043
Newbridge Information Centre, Poundsgate NP
  — 3B **22**, Tel: 01364 631303
Postbridge Information Centre NP — 3A **22**,
  Tel: 01822 880272

Visitor Centre/Information Centre (National Trust)

Boscastle Old Forge Information Centre NT
  — 1C **19**, Tel: 01840 250353
Carnewas (Bedruthan Steps) Information Centre,
  Trenance NT — 1A **12**, Tel: 01637 860563
Heddon Valley Shop Information Centre, Martinhoe
  NT — 2A **34**, Tel: 01598 763402
Plymouth Elizabethan House Information Centre NT
  — Plymouth, Tel: 01752 253871
Selworthy Information Centre NT — 2D **35**
Sexton's Cottage Information Centre, Widecombe in
  the Moor NT — 3B **22**
Trevigue Farm Information Centre NT — 1D **19**,
  Tel: 01840 230418

Watersmeet House Information Centre NT — 2B **34**,
  Tel: 01598 753348

Abbey/Friary/Priory

See also Cathedral, Church

Berry Tower — Bodmin
Buckfast Abbey — 1B **16**
Cleeve Abbey *EH* — 2A **36**
Dunkeswell Abbey — 2B **30**
Exeter St Nicholas Priory — Exeter
Frithelstock Priory — 2C **27**
Launceston St Thomas's Priory — Launceston
Muchelney Abbey *EH* — 1D **31**
Tavistock Abbey — 3C **21**

Animal Collection

See also Farm Park, Wildlife Park, Zoo

Animal Tracks — 1B **28**
Bee World & Animal Centre — 3B **36**
Bolberry Donkey Stud — 3A **16**
Cornwall Donkey & Pony Sanctuary, The — 3C **19**
Dartmoor Otter Sanctuary — 1B **16**
Donkey Sanctuary, The — 2B **24**
Escot Park & Gardens — 1A **24**
Ferne Animal Sanctuary — 3C **31**
Heaven's Gate Farm (Somerset Animal Rescue
  Centre) — 3D **37**
Miniature Pony Centre, The — 2B **22**
Monkey Sanctuary, The — 2A **14**
Mullacott Miniature Ponies & Shire Horse Centre
  — 2D **33**
National Seal Sanctuary — 2B **8**
National Shire Horse Centre, The — 2D **15**
Shaldon Wildlife Trust — 3D **23**
Tamar Otter Sanctuary, The — 2A **20**
Widewalls Animal Sanctuary — 2D **19**

Aquarium

Brixham Aquarium — Brixham
Fowey Aquarium — Fowey
Living Coasts — Torquay
Living from the Sea Aquarium — Looe
Lyme Regis Marine Aquarium (& Cobb History)
  — 1D **25**
Mevagissey Harbour Marine Aquarium — 3C **13**
National Marine Aquarium — Plymouth
Newquay Sea Life Aquarium — Newquay
Weston-super-Mare Sea Life Aquarium — 1D **37**

Arboretum/Botanical Garden

See also Garden

Burrator Reservoir Arboretum — 1D **15**
Eden Project — 2C **13**

Fox Rosehill Gardens — Falmouth
Glenthorne Pinetum — 2B **34**
Homeyards Botanical Gardens, The, Shaldon — 3D 23
Jungleland — 3D **33**
Orchid Paradise — 3C **23**
Pinetum — 1C **15**
Stone Lane Gardens — 1B **22**
Stover Country Park Pinetum, Heathfield — 3C 23
Uplyme Pinetum — 1D **25**

Art Gallery

Burton Art Gallery & Museum — 1C **27**
Byram Gallery, The — 1C **31**
(Camborne Art Gallery, Pool — 1D 7)
Elliott Gallery — 3C **33**
Falmouth Art Gallery — Falmouth
Falmouth Arts Centre — Falmouth
Falmouth College of Arts Gallery — Falmouth
Lakeside Gallery — 3B **20**
Mid-Cornwall Galleries, St Blazey Gate — 2C 13
Newlyn Art Gallery — Penzance
Penwith Galleries — St Ives
Plough Art Gallery, The — 2C **27**
Riverside Mill (The Devon Guild of Craftsmen) — 3C **23**
St Ives Society of Artists — St Ives
Southern Centre, The — 1A **14**
Southgate Gallery — Launceston
Spacex Gallery — Exeter
Tate St Ives — St Ives

Aviary/Bird Garden

Brean Down Tropical Bird Garden — 1C **37**
Cornish Birds of Prey Centre — 1B **12**
Cornish Owl Centre, The — 2B **14**
National Shire Horse Centre Falconry Centre, The, Yealmpton — 2D 15
North Devon Birds of Prey Centre, The — 1B **26**
Paradise Park Wildlife Sanctuary — 2C **7**
Screech Owl Sanctuary — 1B **12**
West Country Falconry Centre, The — 2D **15**

Battle Site

Bovey Heath Battle Site (1646), Bovey Tracey — 3C 23
Fenny Bridges Battle Site (1549) — 1B 24
Langport Battle Site (1645) — 1D 31
Modbury Battle Site (1643) — 2A 16
Sedgemoor Battle Site (1685), Westonzoyland — 3D 37
Stamford Hill Battle Site (1643), Stratton — 3A 26

Bridge

Allerford Packhorse Bridge — 2D 35
Beckford Bridge — 3C **31**
Bellever Clapper Bridge — 3A 22
Bideford Bridge — 1C 27
Bradford Clapper Bridge — 3D **19**
Bury Packhorse Bridge — 1D **29**
Chagford Bridge — 2A 22
Dartmeet Clapper Bridge — 3A **22**
Fingle Bridge — 2B **22**
Gallox Packhorse Bridge *EH* — 2D **35**
Greystone Bridge — 2B **20**
Hellandbridge Bridge — 3C 19
Horner Packhorse Bridge — 2C 35
Horsebridge Bridge — 3A 21
Huntingdon Clapper Bridge — 1A **16**
Ivybridge Viaduct — 2A **16**
Kentsford Packhorse Bridge, Watchet — 2A 36
Landacre Bridge — 3C **35**
Lizwell Packhorse Bridge — 3B **22**
(Lostwithiel Bridge — 2D 13)
Meldon Viaduct — 1D **21**
Moorswater Viaduct — 1A **14**

Pillaton Clapper Bridge — 1B **14**
Postbridge Clapper Bridge — 3A **22**
Powder Mills Clapper Bridge — 3A **22**
Priors Packhorse Bridge — Launceston
Robber's Bridge — 2C **35**
Royal Albert Bridge — 2C **15**
Sidford Packhorse Bridge — 1B 24
Staverton Bridge — 1B 16
Tarr Steps — 3C **35**
Treffry Viaduct — 2C **13**
Wadebridge Bridge — 3B 18
(West Luccombe Packhorse Bridge, Horner — 2C 35
Winsford Packhorse Bridge — 3D **35**
Yeolm Bridge — 2B **20**

Butterfly Farm

Buckfast Butterflies — 1B **16**
Butterfly House of Par Garden Centre, The — 2C **13**
Butterfly House, The — 3D **33**

Castle

See also Castle & Garden, Fortress

Bampton Castle — 1D **29**
Barnstaple Castle — Barnstaple
Berry Pomeroy Castle *EH* — 1C **17**
Blackdown Rings Castle — 2B **16**
Castle Neroche — 2C **31**
Dartmouth Castle *EH* — 2C **17**
Eggesford Castle — 2A **28**
Exeter Rougemont Castle — Exeter
Gidleigh Castle — 2A **22**
Hemyock Castle — 2B **30**
Kilkhampton Castle *NT* — 2A **26**
Launceston Castle *EH* — Launceston
Lydford Castle *EH* — 2D **21**
Nether Stowey Castle — 3B **36**
Okehampton Castle *EH* — 1D **21**
Pendennis Castle *EH* — Falmouth
Plympton Castle — 2D **15**
Restormel Castle *EH* — 1D **13**
St Catherine's Castle *EH* — Fowey
Taunton Castle — Taunton
Tintagel Castle *EH* — 2C **19**
Tiverton Castle — 2D **29**
Totnes Castle *EH* — 1B **16**

Castle & Garden

See also Castle, Fortress

Bickleigh Castle — 3D **29**
Compton Castle *NT* — 1C **17**
Dunster Castle *NT* — 2D **35**
Powderham Castle — 2D **23**
St Mawes Castle *EH* — 1C **9**
St Michael's Mount *NT* — 3C **7**

Cathedral

See also Abbey, Church

Exeter Cathedral — Exeter
Plymouth RC Cathedral — Plymouth
Truro Cathedral — Truro

Church/Chapel/Holy Well

Altarnun St Nonna Church — 2A 20
Bodmin St Petroc Church — Bodmin
Breage St Breaca Church — 3D 7
Brentor St Michael's Church — 2C **21**
Burgundy Chapel — 2D **35**

Chapel of St Lawrence — 1B **16**
Colyton St Andrew's Church — 1C 25
Crewkerne St Bartholomew Church — 3D 31
Culbone St Beuno Church — 2C **35**
Dartmouth St Saviour's Church — Dartmouth
Dupath Holy Well *EH* — 1B **14**
Ilfracombe St Nicholas Chapel — Ilfracombe
Kenton All Saints Church — 2D 23
Launceston St Mary Magdalene Church — Launceston
Loughwood Meeting House *NT* — 1C **25**
Molland St Mary's Church — 1C 29
North Curry St Peter & St Paul Church — 1D 31
Oare Church — 2C **35**
Ottery St Mary Church — 1A 24
Parracombe St Petrock's Church, Churchtown — 2A 34
Plymouth Charles Church — Plymouth
Probus St Probus & St Grace Church — 3A 12
St Cleer Holy Well — 1A **14**
St Clether Holy Well — 2A **20**
St Germans St Germanus Priory Church — 2B **14**
St Ives St Nicholas Chapel — St Ives
St Just-in-Roseland Church — 1C 9
St Keverne St Akeveranus Church — 2B 8
St Keyne Holy Well — 1A **14**
St Madron's Holy Well — 2B **6**
St Neot Holy Well — 1D **13**
St Neot St Anietus Church — 1D 13
Sidbury St Giles' Church — 1B 24
Taunton St Mary Magdalene Church — Taunton
Tawstock Church — 1D 27
Tiverton St Peter's Church — 2D 29
Torbryan Holy Trinity Church — 1C 17
Widecombe in the Moor St Pancras Church — 3B 22
Wolford Chapel — 3B **30**
Zennor St Sennara Church — 2B 6

Cidermaker/Distillery

See also Vineyard

Burrow Hill Cider & the Somerset Cider Brandy Company — 1D **31**
Callestock Cider Farm — 2D **11**
Coombes Somerset Cider — 2D **37**
Countryman Cider — 2B **20**
Hancock's Devon Cider — 1A **28**
Parson's Choice Cider — 1D **31**
Perry's Cider Mills — 2D **37**
Plymouth Gin Distillery — Plymouth
Rich's Farmhouse Cider — 2D **37**
Sheppy's Cider Farm Centre — 1B **30**
Stancombe Cyder — 3B **16**
Tanpits Cider Farm — 1C **31**
Torre Cider Farm — 3A **36**

Country Park

Apex Leisure & Wildlife Park — 2D **37**
Belle Isle Country Park — 1D **23**
Berry Head Country Park — 2D **17**
Cockington Country Park — 1C 17
Combe Sydenham Country Park — 3A **36**
Decoy Country Park — 3C **23**
Grand Western Canal Country Park — 2A **30**
Kit Hill Country Park — 3B **20**
Kitley Caves Country Park, Yealmpton — 2D 15
Mount Edgcumbe Country Park, Cremyll — 2C 15
Northam Burrows Country Park — 3C **33**
River Dart Country Park, The — 3B **22**
Stover Country Park — 3C **23**
Taw Torridge Country Park — 3C **33**
Tehidy Country Park — 1D **7**

Farm Park/Open Farm

See also Animal Collection, Wildlife Park, Zoo

Animal Farm Country Park — 1D **37**
Big Sheep, The — 1C **27**

Blackdown Hills Welcome Centre — 2B **30**
Blagdon Farm — 1B **20**
Bossington Farm & Birds of Prey Centre — 2C **35**
Cheese Farm, The (Lynher Dairies) — 3A **20**
Churchill Farm — 3B **16**
Court Farm Country Park — 1D **37**
Crealy — 1A **24**
Dairyland Farm World — 2A **12**
East Lydeard Country Farm — 1B **30**
Farway Countryside Park — 1B **24**
Fernley's — 3D **19**
Hedgehog Hospital at Prickly Ball Farm — 1C **17**
Home Farm — 2A **36**
North Devon Farm Park — 3A **34**
Old Macdonald's Farm — 3A **18**
Pennywell Farm — 1B **16**
Roskilly's — 2B **8**
Secret World (Badger & Wildlife Rescue Centre) — 2D **37**
Shire Horse Farm, The — 2D **7**
Sorley Tunnel Adventure Farm — 3B **16**
Tamar Valley Donkey Park, The — 3C **21**
Tordown Farm — 3A **34**
Trenouth Farm Rare Breeds Centre — 3B **18**
Trethorne Leisure Farm — 2A **20**
World of Country Life, The — 2A **24**

Forest Walk/Nature Trail

See also Nature Reserve

Abbeyford Woods Forest Walks — 1D **21**
Aisholt Ring Walk — 3B **36**
Argal & College Reservoirs Walks — 1B **8**
Arlington Court Nature Walk *NT* — 2A **34**
Ashclyst Forest Walks — 1A **24**
Aylesbeare Common Nature Trail — 2A **24**
Becky Falls Nature Trails — 3B **22**
Bellever Forest Forest Walks — 3A **22**
Berry Head Country Park Nature Trail, Brixham — 2D 17
Bincombe Beeches Nature Trail — 2D **31**
Blagdon Farm Nature Trail — 1B **20**
Bolberry Down Nature Trail *NT* — 3A **16**
Bullers Hill Forest Walks, Kennford — 2C 23
Bullers Hill Forest Walks — 2C **23**
Burrator Reservoir Woodland Walks — 1D **15**
Burridge Woodland Trail, Dulverton — 1D 29
Cann Wood Forest Walk — 2D **15**
Canonteign Falls Nature Trails — 2C **23**
Cardinham Woods Forest Walks — 1C **13**
Cardinham Woods Forest Walks — 1D **13**
Castle Neroche Nature Trail — 2C **31**
Chapel Porth Nature Trail — 1D **7**
Chapel Wood Nature Trails — 2C **33**
Chard Reservoir Walk — 3D **31**
Clatworthy Reservoir Nature Trail — 3A **36**
Cloutsham Woodland Trail *NT* — 2D **35**
Colliford Lake Walks — 3D **19**
Combe Sydenham Country Park Woodland Walks — 3A **36**
Cookworthy Moor Plantation Forest Walk — 3C **27**
Coombe Valley Nature Trail — 2A **26**
Cotehele Woodland Walks, St Dominick NT — 1C 15
Cothelstone Hill Trail — 3B **36**
Dead Woman's Ditch Trail — 3B **36**
Decoy Country Park Woodland Walks — 3C **23**
Deerpark Forest Forest Trail — 1D **13**
Denham Forest Walk — 1C **15**
East Hill Woodland Walk — 1B **24**
Fernworthy Forest Walks — 2A **22**
Five Pond Wood Trail — 1C **31**
Fyne Court Nature Trails — 3C **37**
Gaff & Undertown Woodland Walk — 1C **13**
Glenthorne Estate Walks, Countisbury — 2B 34
Great Wood Walk — 3B **36**
Hall Walk *NT* — Fowey
Halsdon Nature Trails — 2D **27**

Heddon Valley Nature Walk *NT* — 2A **34**
Hembury Nature Trail, Buckfast NT — 1B 16
Herne Hill Nature Trail — 2D **31**
Herodsfoot Woods Forest Trails — 2A **14**
Heywood Forest Walk — 2A **28**
Higher Moors Nature Trail, St Mary's, Isles of Scilly — 1B 66
Hilltown Wood Forest Walks — 2A **28**
Hinkley Point Nature Trail — 2C **37**
Holsworthy Woods Forest Walk — 3B **26**
Horner Wood Woodland Walks *NT* — 2C **35**
Hurscombe Nature Trail — 3D **35**
Idless Wood Forest Walks — 3A **12**
Kelly Bray Forest Trail — 3B 20
Kilminorth Woods Forest Walks — 2A **14**
Kit Hill Walk — 3B **20**
Kitley Caves Country Park Woodland Trail, Yealmpton — 2D 15
Lanhydrock Nature Walks, Cutmadoc NT — 1C 13
Longtimber & Pithill Woods Woodland Walks, Ivybridge — 2A 16
Lower Moors Nature Trail, Old Town, St Mary's, Isles of Scilly — 1B 66
Lydford Forest Trail — 2C **21**
Mamhead Forest Walk — 2D **23**
Mellingey Mill Woodland Walk — 3B 18
North Hill Woodland Trail — 2D **35**
Nutcombe Bottom Forest Trails — 2D **35**
Otterhead Lakes Nature Walk — 2C **31**
Pendarves Wood Nature Trail — 2D **7**
Penrose Estate (Loe Pool Nature) Walks *NT* — 3D **7**
Plym Bridge Riverside & Woodland Walks *NT* — 2D **15**
Quantock Forest Trail — 3B **36**
Red & Southern Red Moors Nature Trail — 1C **13**
Restormel Woodland Trail, Lostwithiel — 1D 13
River Dart Country Park Nature & Tree Trails — 3B **22**
Roadford Lake Walks — 1C **21**
St Anthony-in-Roseland Nature Walk *NT* — 1C **9**
Salcombe Hill Nature Trail — 2B **24**
Siblyback Lake Walks, St Cleer — 3A 20
Simpson Farm Nature Trail — 3B **26**
Slapton Ley Nature Trail — 3C 17
Staple Plain Trails *NT* — 2B **36**
Steps Bridge Nature Trail *NT* — 2C **23**
Stoke Woods Forest Walks — 1D **23**
Strete Gate Nature Trail — 3C **17**
Swell Wood Woodland Trail — 1D **31**
Tamar Lakes Nature Trail — 2A **26**
Tamar Valley Nature Trails — 1C **15**
Tehidy Country Park Woodland Trails, Portreath — 1D 7
Teign Gorge Walk *NT* — 1B **22**
Thorne Farm Nature Trail — 3B **26**
Town Tree Nature Trail — 1D **31**
Tregassick Nature Walk *NT* — 1C **9**
Tregellast Barton Nature Trails — 2B **8**
Trelissick Woodland Walk NT — 1C 9
Trelowarren Woodland Walk, Garras — 2B 8
Trenchford & Tottiford Reservoir Walks, Lustleigh — 2C 23
Treworgie Barton Woodland Trails — 1D **19**
Weston Woods Nature Trail — 1D **37**
Wistlandpound Reservoir Nature Trail, Blackmoor Gate — 2A 34
Yarner Wood Nature Trails — 3B **22**

Fortress

See also Castle, Castle & Garden

Bayard's Cove Fort *EH* — Dartmouth
Berry Head Fortifications, Brixham — 2D 17
Brean Down Fort — 1C **37**
Chudleigh Fort — 1C **27**
(Crab Quay Battery, Falmouth — 1C 9)
Cromwell's Castle — 1A **66**
Crownhill Fort — 2C **15**
Fort Charles, Salcombe — 3B 16
Fowey Blockhouse — Fowey
Garrison Walls *EH* — 2A **66**
Harry's Walls, Hugh Town, St Mary's, Isles of Scilly EH — 1B 66
King Charles's Castle — 1A **66**
(Little Dennis Blockhouse, Falmouth — 1C 9)
Old Blockhouse, Tresco, Isles of Scilly EH — 1A 66
Plymouth Breakwater Fort — 2C 15

Polruan Blockhouse — Fowey
Royal Citadel, The *EH* — Plymouth
St Anthony Battery NT — 1C 9
Star Castle — 1A **66**

Garden

See also Arboretum, Historic Building & Garden

Antony Woodland Garden — 2C **15**
Ashford Gardens — 3D **33**
Avenue Cottage Gardens — 2C **17**
Bickham Barton Gardens — 1C **15**
Bicton College Garden & Arboretum — 2A **24**
Bicton Park & Pleasure Gardens — 2A **24**
Bosvigo Garden — Truro
Burncoose Nurseries Garden — 1B **8**
Burrow Farm Gardens — 1C **25**
Cannington College Heritage Gardens — 3C **37**
Carreg Dhu Gardens — 1B **66**
Carwinion Garden — 2B **8**
Catchfrench Manor Gardens — 2B **14**
Clapton Court Gardens — 3D **31**
Cockington Court Gardens — 1C **17**
Coleton Fishacre Garden *NT* — 2D **17**
Cothay Manor Garden — 1A **30**
Creed House Garden — 3B **12**
Dartington Hall Gardens — 1B **16**
Docton Mill Gardens — 1A **26**
Downes Garden, The — 1C **27**
East Lambrook Manor Garden — 2D **31**
Elworthy Cottage Garden — 3A **36**
Endsleigh House Gardens — 3B **20**
Garden House, The — 1C **15**
Gate House Gardens, The — 2C **33**
Glendurgan Garden *NT* — 2B **8**
Greencombe Garden, West Porlock — 2C 35
Gyllyngdune Gardens — Falmouth
Headland Garden — Fowey
Hestercombe Formal & Landscape Gardens — 1C **31**
Hill House Gardens — 1B **16**
Japanese Garden, The — 1A **12**
Kelways Cottage Gardens — 1D **31**
Ken-Caro Garden — 1B **14**
Kentsford House Gardens — 2C **15**
Lamorran House Garden, St Mawes — 1C 9
Lanterns Garden — 1C **9**
Little Upcott Gardens — 1A **24**
Longcross Victorian Gardens — 3B **18**
Lost Gardens of Heligan, The — 3B **12**
Lower Severalls Garden — 2D **31**
Lukesland Gardens — 2A **16**
Marshford Organic Nursery Garden — 1C **27**
Marwood Hill Gardens — 3D **33**
Maunsel House Gardens — 3D **37**
Mount Edgcumbe Country Park Formal Gardens, Cremyll — 2C 15
Old Mill Herbary, The — 3C **19**
Overbeck's Garden *NT* — 3B **16**
Penjerrick Gardens — 1B **8**
Pine Lodge Gardens, St Austell — 2C **13**
Plant World — 1C **17**
Pleasant View Nursery Garden — 1C **17**
Probus Gardens — 3B **12**
Rock Gardens, The — 3C **23**
Rosemoor Garden (The Royal Horticultural Society) — 2C **13**
Tapeley Park Gardens — 1C **27**
Tehidy Country Park Rose Garden — 1D **7**
Towan Nurseries Camellia Garden — 1C **9**
Trebah Garden — 2B **8**
Tregrehan — 2C **13**
Trelissick Garden NT — 1C 9
Tremeer Gardens — 3C **19**
Trenance Gardens — Newquay
Trengwainton Garden NT — 2B 6
Tresco Abbey Gardens — 1A **66**
Trevarno Estate & Gardens — 2D **7**
Wetherham Gardens — 3C **19**
Woodland Garden — 2B **8**

Hill Fort

See also Prehistoric Monument

Bat's Castle — 2D **35**

Kents Cavern — 1D **17**
Kitley Caves — 2D **15**
Piper's Hole — 1A **66**
Poldark Mine — 2D **7**
Rosevale Mine — 2A **6**
Vitifer Tin Mine — 2A **22**

Monument/Folly

Augustus Smith Monument — 1A **66**
Basset Monument — 1D **7**
Bishop's Tower — 3B **30**
Blackmore Memorial — 2B **34**
Burton Pynsent Monument — 1D **31**
Charlotte Dymond Monument — 2D **19**
Col. R.H. Maclaren Memorial — 2B **34**
Compass Point Storm Tower — Bude
Conygar Tower, Dunster — 2D 35
Devonport Column — 2C **15**
Doyden Castle *NT* — 2B **18**
Drake's Statue — Plymouth
Fortescue Monument — 3B **34**
Gilbert Monument — Bodmin
Goathurst Churchyard Monument — 3C **37**
Grylls Monument — 3D **7**
Hancock Memorial Stone — 1C **29**
Hatherleigh Obelisk — 3D **27**
HMS Anson Monument *NT* — 3D **7**
King Alfred's Monument — 1D **31**
Knill's Monument — 2C **7**
Lander Monument — Truro
Lawrence Castle (Haldon Belvedere) — 2C **23**
Letterbox Memorial — 1A **16**
Lord Antrim Memorial — 1D **25**
Mamhead Obelisk, Ashcombe — 2D 23
Marconi Monument *NT* — 3D **7**
Mayflower Stone & Steps — Plymouth
Normandy Landings Obelisk — 3C **17**
Plymouth Naval Cenotaph — Plymouth
St Piran's Oratory Monument — 2D **11**
Scott Memorial — 2C **15**
Sedgemoor Battle Monument — 3D **37**
Sharrow Grotto *NT* — 2B **14**
Sherman Tank Memorial — 3C **17**
Sir Arthur Quiller-Couch Memorial *NT* — Fowey
*Sir Cloudesley Shovell Monument, St Mary's,
  Isles of Scilly — 1B 66*
Temple of Harmony — 3C **37**
Ten Commandments Stone, The — 3B **22**
Wellington Monument *NT* — 2B **30**

Museum

Admiral Blake Museum — 3D **37**
Allhallows Museum, Honiton — 3B 30
Ashburton Museum — 1B 16
Automobilia (Cornwall's Motor Museum) — 2B **12**
Axbridge Museum — 1D 37
Axe Valley Heritage Museum — 1C **25**
Axminster Museum — 1C **25**
Bakelite Museum (Orchard Mill Museum)
  — 2A **36**
Barbara Hepworth Museum & Sculpture Garden
  — St Ives
Barometer World & Museum — 2D **27**
Bideford Railway Station Museum — 1C **27**
Bishopsteignton Museum of Rural Life — 3D **23**
Blazes The Fire Museum — 1B **30**
Blue Anchor Station Great Western Railway Museum
  — 2A **36**
Bodmin Museum — Bodmin
Bowden House Photographic Museum — 2C **17**
Brannams Pottery & Museum — 3D **33**
Braunton & District Museum — 3C **33**
British Cycling Museum — 2D **19**
Brixham Museum — Brixham
Bude-Stratton Museum — Bude
'Bygones' — 1D **17**
Callestock Cider Farm Museum — 2D **11**
Callington Museum — 1B **14**
Camborne Museum — 2D 7
Camborne School of Mines Geological Museum
  — 1D **7**
'Century of Playtime' Doll & Toy Museum — Paignton

Chard & District Museum — 3D **31**
Charlestown Shipwreck, Rescue & Heritage Centre
  — 2C **13**
Clovelly Fisherman's Cottage — 1B **26**
Clovelly Lifeboat Museum — 1B **26**
Cobbaton Combat Collection — 1A **28**
Coldharbour Mill (Working Wool) Industrial Museum
  — 2A **30**
Combe Martin Motorcycle Collection, The — 2D **33**
Combe Martin Museum — 2D **33**
Cookworthy Museum, The — 3B **16**
Copeland China Collection — 1C **9**
Cornish Methodism, Museum of — 3D **11**
Cornwall Geological Museum — Penzance
Cotehele Quay Museum (National Maritime
  Museum Outstation) *NT* — 1C **15**
Crowcombe Heathfield Station Permanent Way
  Exhibition — 3B **36**
Croyde Gem, Rock & Shell Museum — 3C **33**
Dartmoor Life, Museum of — 1D **21**
Dartmouth Museum — Dartmouth
Dawlish Museum — 3D **23**
Delabole Slate Quarry Display Room — 2C **19**
Dingles Steam Village — 2C **21**
Dinosaurland — 1D **25**
Duke of Cornwall's Light Infantry Museum
  — Bodmin
Dunster Dolls Museum, The — 2D 35
Exmouth Museum — 2A **24**
Fairlynch Museum & Arts Centre — 2A **24**
Forgotten World (The Wheelwright's &
  Romany Museum) — 1D **37**
Fowey Museum — Fowey
Geevor Tin Mine Heritage Centre — 2A **6**
Hartland Quay Museum — 1A **26**
Helicopter Museum, The — 1D **37**
Helston Folk Museum — 3D **7**
Holsworthy Local History Museum — 3B 26
Ilfracombe Museum — Ilfracombe
*Isles of Scilly Museum, Hugh Town, St Mary's,
  Isles of Scilly — 1B 66*
James Countryside Museum — 2A **24**
John Betjeman Centre, Wadebridge — 3B 18
Kingsley Museum — 1B **26**
Kitley Caves Museum, Yealmpton — 2D 15
Lanreath Folk & Farm Museum — 2D **13**
Launceston Steam Railway Transport Museum
  — Launceston
Lawnmower Museum, The *NT* — 2A **12**
Lawrence House Museum *NT* — Launceston
Liskeard Town Museum — Liskeard
Lostwithiel Museum — 2D **13**
Lyme Regis Philpot Museum — 1D **25**
Lyn & Exmoor Museum — Lynton & Lynmouth
Lynmouth Flood Exhibition — Lynton & Lynmouth
Marazion Museum — 2C 7
Mellingey Mill Willow Craft Centre — 3B **18**
Merlin's Cave Crystal, Mineral & Fossil Museum
  — 2C **19**
Mevagissey Folk Museum — 3C **13**
Morwellham Quay — 1C **15**
National Ambulance Heritage Centre — 3D **21**
National Maritime Museum Cornwall — Falmouth
National Museum of Baking — 3A **36**
Newton Abbot Town & Great Western Railway
  Museum — Newton Abbot
North Cornwall Museum & Gallery — 2D **19**
North Devon Maritime Museum — 3C **33**
North Devon, The Museum of (Museum on the
  Square) — Barnstaple
Old Bakery, The *NT* — 2B **24**
Old Guildhall Museum, The — Looe
Otterton Mill Museum — 2A **24**
Overbeck's Museum *NT* — 3B **16**
Pack O' Cards Inn Museum — 2D **33**
Padstow Museum — Padstow
Paul Corin's Magnificent Music Machines — 1A **14**
Penlee House Gallery & Museum — Penzance
Penryn Museum — 1B 8
Penzance Maritime Museum — Penzance
Perranzabuloe Folk Museum — 2D **11**
Perry's Cider Mills Museum — 2D **31**
Piers Museum — Paignton
Plymouth City Museum & Art Gallery — Plymouth
Plymouth Merchant's House Museum — Plymouth
Poldark Mine Heritage Complex, The — 2D **7**
Polperro Heritage Museum of Smuggling & Fishing
  — 2A **14**

Porlock Museum — 2C 35
Portreath & its Tramroads Exhibition — 1D **7**
Power of Water Exhibition — Lynton & Lynmouth
Prehistoric Hill Settlement Museum — 2C **17**
Rowena Cade Exhibition Centre — 3A **6**
Royal Albert Memorial Museum & Art Gallery
  — Exeter
Royal Cornwall Museum — Truro
St Agnes Museum — 2D 11
St Ives Museum — St Ives
St Winnow Barton Farm Museum — 2D **13**
Salcombe Maritime & Local History Museum
  — 3B **16**
Salcombe RNLI Museum — 3B **16**
Sheppy's Cider Farm & Cider Museum — 1B **30**
Shire Horse Farm Carriage Museum, The — 2D **7**
Sidmouth Museum — 2B **24**
Somerset & Dorset Railway Trust Museum — 2A **36**
Somerset Brick & Tile Museum — 3D **37**
Somerset County Museum — Taunton
Somerset Cricket Museum — Taunton
Somerset Military Museum, The — Taunton
South Devon Railway Museum — 1B **16**
South Molton Museum — 1B **28**
Submarine Telegraphy, Museum of — 3A **6**
Tavistock Museum — 3C **21**
Teignmouth Museum — 3D **23**
'The Bunker' Underground Military Museum
  — 2D **37**
Time Machine, The — 1D **37**
Tintagel Toy Museum — 2C 19
Tiverton Museum — 2D **29**
Topsham Museum — 2D **23**
Torquay Museum — Torquay
Torrington Museum, Great Torrington — 2C 27
Totnes Costume Museum (Devonshire Collection
  of Period Costume) — 1C **17**
Totnes (Elizabethan) Museum — 1C 17
Trenance Heritage Cottages — Newquay
Trevarno Estate Gardening Museum — 2D **7**
Trinity House National Lighthouse Centre
  — Penzance
Valhalla Figurehead Collection — 1A **66**
Vintage Toy & Train Museum, The — 2B **24**
Watchet Market House Museum — 2A **36**
Waterpower, Museum of *NT* — 1A **22**
Wayside Folk Museum, The — 2B **6**
Wellington Museum — 1B **30**
*West Somerset Rural Life Museum, The, Allerford
  — 2D 35*
Wheal Martyn China Clay Heritage Centre — 2C **13**
Whimple Dollshouse & Toy Museum — 1A **24**
Willows & Wetlands Visitor Centre — 1D **31**
Wireless in the West, Washford — 2A 36
World of Country Life Museum, The — 2A **24**
Yelverton Paperweight Centre — 1D 15

Natural Attraction

Becky Falls — 3B **22**
Bedruthan Steps — 1A **12**
Blackingstone Rock — 2B **22**
Bowerman's Nose — 2B **22**
Bowl Rock *NT* — 2C **7**
Burrow Mump *NT* — 3D **37**
Canonteign Falls — 2C **23**
Cape Cornwall *NT* — 2A **6**
Chains, The — 2B **34**
Cheesewring, The — 3A **20**
Chudleigh Rock — 3C 23
Countisbury Cliffs *NT* — 1B **34**
Cranmere Pool — 2A **22**
Dartmeet — 3A **22**
Devil's Bellows Blow-hole *NT* — 1C **19**
Devil's Bellows Blow-hole — 3A **8**
Devil's Cauldron *NT* — 2D **21**
Devil's Frying Pan *NT* — 3B **8**
Devil's Jump — 3D **19**
Devil's Limekiln *NT* — 2A **32**
Devil's Slide — 3A **32**
Dewerstone Rock, The *NT* — 1D **15**
Giant's Rock — 3D **7**
Glen Lyn Gorge — Lynton & Lynmouth
Golden Cap Cliffs *NT* — 1D **25**
Golitha Falls — 1A **14**

Great Mis Tor — 3D **21**
Great Staple Tor — 3D **21**
Haytor Rocks — 3B **22**
Heddon's Cleave & Mouth *NT* — 2A **34**
Hell's Mouth *NT* — 1D **7**
High Cliff *NT* — 1D **19**
High Willhays — 2D **21**
Hound Tor — 3B **22**
Kynance Cove *NT* — 3A **8**
Land's End — 3A **6**
Lion's Den — 3B **8**
Little Hangman *NT* — 2D **33**
Lizard Point — 3B **8**
Loe Pool & Bar *NT* — 3D **7**
Logan Rock — 3A **6**
Logan Stone — 2B **66**
Lowland Point Raised Beach *NT* — 3C **9**
Lustleigh Cleave — 2B **22**
Lydford Gorge *NT* — 2D **21**
Nag's Head, St Agnes, Isles of Scilly — 2A **66**
Peninnis Head Blow-hole — 2B **66**
Pulpit Rock — 2B **66**
Punch Bowl — 2A **66**
Ralph's Cupboard *NT* — 1D **7**
Roche Rock — 2B **12**
Rocky Valley — 2C **19**
Roughtor *NT* — 2D **19**
St Nectan's Glen — 2C **19**
Speke's Mill Mouth Waterfall — 1A **26**
Tavy Cleave — 2D **21**
Tunnels Beach — Ilfracombe
Valley of Rocks, The — Lynton & Lynmouth
Vixen Tor — 3D **21**
Watersmeet *NT* — 2B **34**
White Lady Waterfall *NT* — 2D **21**
Yes Tor — 1D **21**

Nature Reserve/Bird Sanctuary (English Nature, RSPB, The Wildfowl & Wetlands Trust, selected only)

See also Forest Walk

Axmouth-Lyme Undercliffs Nature Reserve — 1D **25**
Aylesbeare Common Nature Reserve — 1A **24**
Berrow Dunes Nature Reserve — 1C **37**
Black Tor Copse Nature Reserve — 2D **21**
Bovey Valley Woodlands Nature Reserve — 3B **22**
Bowling Green Marsh Bird Sanctuary, Topsham — 2D **23**
Braunton Burrows Nature Reserve — 3C **33**
Brean Down Bird Sanctuary *NT* — 1C **37**
Breney Common Nature Reserve — 1C **13**
Bridgwater Bay Bird Sanctuary — 2C **37**
Camel Estuary Bird Sanctuary, Wadebridge — 3B **18**
Chapel Wood Bird Sanctuary — 2C **33**
Chard Reservoir Nature Reserve — 3D **31**
Dart Valley Nature Reserve — 3A **22**
Dawlish Warren Local Nature Reserve — 3D **23**
Dunsford & Meadhaydown Woods Nature Reserve *NT* — 2B **22**
Exminster Marshes Bird Sanctuary — 2D **23**
Fernworthy Reservoir Bird Sanctuary, Chagford — 2A **22**
Fyne Court Nature Reserve — 3C **37**
Golitha Nature Reserve, St Cleer — 1A **14**
Hayle Estuary Bird Sanctuary — 2C **7**
Horner Wood Nature Reserve *NT* — 2C **35**
Isley Marshes Bird Sanctuary — 3C **33**
Langford Heathfield Nature Reserve — 1A **30**
Lizard Nature Reserve, The — 3A **8**
Marazion Marsh Bird Sanctuary — 2C **7**
Red & Southern Red Moors Nature Reserve — 1C **13**
Shapwick Heath Nature Reserve — 2D **37**
Slapton Ley Bird Sanctuary — 3C **17**
Steep Holm Nature Reserve — 1C **37**
Stithians Reservoir Bird Sanctuary, Penhalvean — 1B **8**
Swell Wood Bird Sanctuary — 1D **31**
Tamar Valley Wildlife Reserve — 1C **15**
Town Tree Nature Gardens & Reserve — 1D **31**
Wembury Marine Conservation Area — 3C **15**
Westhay Moor Nature Reserve — 2D **37**
West Sedgemoor Bird Sanctuary — 1D **31**
Wistman's Wood Nature Reserve — 3A **22**
Yarner Wood Nature Reserve — 3B **22**

Place of Interest (General)

Appledore Lifeboat Station — 3C **33**
ATV Centre, The — 3D **11**
Babbacombe Model Village — 1D **17**
Barnstaple Heritage Centre — Barnstaple
Bennett's Cross — 2A **22**
Bens Play World — 2C **13**
Billingsmoor Farm — 3D **29**
Bird of Prey Viewpoint — 2C **23**
Bishopsteignton Bishop's Palace — 3D **23**
Bodmin Jail — Bodmin
Bodmin Shire Hall Court Room Experience — Bodmin
Boringdon Gate Piers *NT* — 2D **15**
Bowdens Farm Smokery — 1D **31**
Bowhill *EH* — 1D **23**
Braunton Great Field — 3C **33**
Broadwindsor Craft & Design Centre — 3D **31**
Bude Haven Lifeboat Station — Bude
Camelford Town Hall — 2D **19**
Caratacus Stone *NT* — 3C **35**
Cardew Teapottery — 3C **23**
Cardinham Cross — 1D **13**
Catacombs, The — Exeter
Colyford Filling Station — 1C **25**
Cornwall Pearl — 1A **12**
Cornworthy St Mary's Priory Gatehouse — 2C **17**
Crewkerne Heritage Centre — 3D **31**
Dartington Cider Press Centre — 1B **16**
Dartington Crystal — 2C **27**
Dartmoor Prison — 3D **21**
Day Mark, The — 1B **66**
Deep, The — Brixham
Delabole Slate Quarry — 2C **19**
Delabole Wind Farm — 2C **19**
Devon County Showground — 1D **23**
Doone Valley — 2B **34**
Dozmary Pool — 3D **19**
Dulverton Guildhall Heritage Centre — 1D **29**
Dungeons, The — 2C **7**
Dunster Butter Cross *EH* — 2D **35**
Eastacott Cross — 1A **28**
Exeter City Walls — Exeter
Exeter Underground Passages — Exeter
Exmoor Brass Rubbing Centre — Lynton & Lynmouth
Exmoor Natural History Centre — 2B **34**
Exmouth Lifeboat Station — 2A **24**
Flitton Oak — 3B **34**
(Fosters Pottery, Pool — 1D 7)
Gnome Reserve & Wild Flower Garden, The — 2B **26**
Golden Hind, The — Brixham
Goonhilly Earth Station — 2B **8**
Grand Pier, The — 3D **23**
Great Exmouth OO Model Railway, The — 2A **24**
Great Weston Train Experience, The — 1D **37**
Gribbin Daymark *NT* — 3C **13**
Gwennap Pit — 3D **11**
Hawker's Hut *NT* — 2A **26**
Hayes Barton — 2A **24**
Heddon Oak — 3B **36**
Hidden Valley Nature World (Tredidon Trails) — 2A **20**
Hinkley Point Power Stations — 2C **37**
Hoar Oak Tree — 2B **34**
Hobby Drive — 1B **26**
Hound Tor Deserted Medieval Village *EH* — 3B **22**
House of Marbles & Teign Valley Glass — 3C **23**
Ilfracombe Lifeboat Station — Ilfracombe
Instow Signal Box — 3C **33**
Jamaica Inn — 3D **19**
Jubilee Rock — 3D **19**
Kidscove — 1D **37**
Kids Kingdom — 2C **13**
Kilve Chantry — 2B **36**
King Arthur's Great Halls — 2C **19**
King Doniert's Stone *EH* — 1A **14**
Kingsbury Episcopal Lock-up — 1D **31**
King's Pipe — Falmouth
Lamorna Pottery — 3B **6**
Land's End — 3A **6**
Leigh Barton *EH* — 3B **16**
Lizard Lifeboat Station, The — 3B **8**
Looe Lifeboat Station — Looe
Look 3D — 1D **19**
Lyme Regis Lifeboat Station — 1D **25**

Marazion Lifeboat Station — 3C **7**
Minack Open-Air Theatre, The — 3A **6**
Minehead Lifeboat Station — Minehead
Minions Cross — 3A **20**
(Minions Heritage Centre — 3A 20)
Moretonhampstead Almshouses *NT* — 2B **22**
Mortehoe Heritage Centre — 2C **33**
Mylor Cross — 1C **9**
Newquay Lifeboat Station — Newquay
Norman Lockyer Observatory — 2B **24**
Old Mill, The *NT* — 3D **15**
Padstow Lifeboat Station — 3A **18**
Paignton Pier — Paignton
Pecorama — 2C **25**
Penlee Lifeboat Station — 3B **6**
Pilchard Works, The — Penzance
Pipe Well — Liskeard
Plymouth Dome — Plymouth
Plymouth Lifeboat Station — Plymouth
Polperro Model Village & Land of Legend — 2A **14**
Porlock Scenic Toll Road — 2C **35**
Porlock Weir Scenic Toll Road — 2C **35**
Porteath Bee Centre — 3B **18**
Port Isaac Lifeboat Station — 2B **18**
Quince Honey Farm — 1B **28**
RNAS Culdrose Viewing Enclosure — 3D **7**
Rock Lifeboat Station — 3B **18**
Royal Cornwall Showground — 3B **18**
St Agnes Lifeboat Station — 2D **11**
St Ives Lifeboat Station — St Ives
St Just Playing Place Amphitheatre — 2A **6**
St Warna's Well — 2A **66**
Sennen Cove Lifeboat Station — 3A **6**
Slaughterbridge — 2D **19**
Sloley Stone — 3B **34**
Smugglers at Jamaica Inn — 3D **19**
Square Sail Shipyard — 2C **13**
Tawstock Gatehouse — 1D **27**
(Teignmouth Lifeboat Station — 3D 23)
Tommy Taylor's — Taunton
Triscombe Stone — 3B **36**
Tristan Stone — 2D **13**
Troy Town Maze — 2A **66**
Tuckers Maltings — Newton Abbot
Tunnels Through Time — Newquay
Veryan Round Houses — 1D **9**
Weston-super-Mare Grand Pier — 1D **37**
Weston-super-Mare Heritage Centre — 1D **37**
Westworld Raceway — 1B **12**
White Rock — 1A **22**
Whit Stones — 2C **35**
World in Miniature — 2D **11**
World of Model Railways — 3C **13**

Prehistoric Monument

See also Hill Fort

Alderman's Barrow *NT* — 2C **35**
Ballowall Barrow *EH* — 2A **6**
Bant's Carn Burial Chamber *EH* — 1B **66**
Blind Fiddler Standing Stone, The — 3B **6**
Boscawen-un Stone Circle — 3B **6**
Boswens Standing Stone — 2B **6**
Brown Gelly Barrows — 3D **19**
Brown Gelly Settlements — 3A **20**
Butterdon Stone Row — 2A **16**
Carne Beacon (Veryan Barrow) — 1D **9**
Carn Euny Ancient Village *EH* — 3B **6**
Castlewich Henge — 1B **14**
Chapman Barrows — 2A **34**
Chun Quoit — 2B **6**
Chysauster Ancient Village *EH* — 2B **6**
Corringdon Ball Long Barrow — 1A **16**
Craddock Moor Stone Circle — 3A **20**
Duloe Stone Circle — 2A **14**
Farway Hill Barrows — 1B **24**
Fernacre Stone Circle — 3D **19**
Fernworthy Forest Stone Circle — 2A **22**
Five Barrows — 3B **34**
Foales Arrishes Settlement — 3B **22**
Giant's Quoits — 3A **6**
Grey Wethers Stone Circles — 2A **22**
Grimspound *EH* — 2B **22**

Halangy Down Ancient Village, St Mary's,
    Isles of Scilly EH — 1B **66**
Halliggye Fogou EH — 2B **8**
Hall Rings — 2A **14**
Hamel Down Barrows — 3B **22**
Hurlers Stone Circles, The EH — 3A **20**
Innisidgen Lower & Upper Burial Chambers EH
    — 1B **66**
Joaney How & Robin How Burial Cairns — 2D **35**
Kestor Settlement — 2A **22**
King Arthur's Hall — 3D **19**
Lanyon Quoit NT — 2B **6**
Longstone — 2B **34**
Magi Stone — 1B **12**
Meare Lake Villages (site of) — 2D **37**
Men-an-Tol — 2B **6**
Men Scryfa Inscribed Stone — 2B **6**
Merrivale Prehistoric Settlement EH — 3D **21**
Merry Maidens Stone Circle — 3B **6**
Mulfra Quoit — 2B **6**
Nine Maidens Stone Circle — 2B **6**
Nine Maidens Stone Row — 1B **12**
Old Man of Gugh, Gugh, Isles of Scilly — 2A **66**
Pawton Quoit — 1B **12**
Pipers Standing Stones, The — 3B **6**
Porlock Stone Circle — 2C **35**
Porth Hellick Down Burial Chamber EH — 1B **66**
Rider's Rings Enclosures — 1A **16**
Rillaton Barrow — 3A **20**
Robin Hood's Butts — 2C **31**
Roughtor Hut Circles — 2D **19**
St Breock Downs Monolith EH — 1B **12**
St Piran's Round (Perran Round) — 2D **11**
Scorhill Stone Circle — 2A **22**
Setta Barrow — 3B **34**
Shovel Down Stone Rows — 2A **22**
Sperris Quoit — 2B **6**
Spinster's Rock Burial Chamber — 1B **22**
Stall Moor Stone Row — 1A **16**
Stannon Stone Circle — 3D **19**
Stripple Stones Henge & Circle — 3D **19**
Tregiffian Burial Chamber EH — 3B **6**
Trethevy Quoit EH — 1A **14**
Trippet Stones Circle — 3D **19**
Upper Plym Valley Prehistoric Sites EH — 1D **15**
Wambarrows — 3C **35**
Zennor Quoit — 2B **6**

Railway (Heritage, Narrow Gauge, Miniature)

Beer Heights Light Railway — 2C **25**
Bickington Steam Railway — 3C **23**
Bicton Woodland Railway, East Budleigh — 2A **24**
Bodmin & Wenford Railway — 1C **13** to 1D **13**
Brean Central Miniature Railway — 1C **37**
Buckfastleigh Miniature Railway — 1B **16**
Combe Martin Wildlife Park Railway — 2D **33**
Cricket St Thomas Railway — 3D **31**
Dartmoor Railway — 1D **21**
Devon Railway Centre — 3D **29**
Dobwalls Miniature Railroad — 1A **14**
Exmoor Steam Railway — 3A **34**
Exmouth Express — 2A **24**
Gorse Blossom Miniature Railway & Woodland Park
    — 3C **23**
Great Torrington Railway — 2D **27**
Jungle Express, Paignton — 2C **17**
Lappa Valley Steam Railway — 2A **12**
Launceston Steam Railway — 2B **20**
Little Western Railway — Newquay
Lynbarn Railway, The — 1B **26**
Lynton & Lynmouth Cliff Railway
    — Lynton & Lynmouth

Oddicombe Cliff Railway — 1D **17**
Paignton & Dartmouth Steam Railway
    — 1C **17** to 2C **17**
Paradise Railway — 2C **7**
Pixieland Miniature Railway — 2A **26**
Plym Valley Railway (Woodland Line) — 2D **15**
Seaton Tramway — 1C **25**
South Devon Railway (Primrose Line) — 1B **16** to 1C **17**
Tamarisk Miniature Railway — 3A **18**
Weston Miniature Railway — 1D **37**
West Somerset Railway — 1B **30** to 2D **35**

Roman Remains

Martinhoe Beacon Roman Fortlet NT — 2A **34**
Old Burrow Roman Fortlet — 2B **34**

Spot Height

Brown Willy 420 m (1377 ft) — 3D **19**
Dunkery Beacon 519 m (1704 ft) NT — 2C **35**
Golden Cap 191 m (627 ft) — 1D **25**
High Willhays 621 m (2038 ft) — 2D **21**
Pilsdon Pen 277 m (909 ft) NT — 3D **31**
Telegraph Hill 51 m (167 ft), St Mary's,
    Isles of Scilly — 1B **66**
Western Common 493 m (1617 ft) — 3B **34**
Wills Neck 384 m (1260 ft) — 3B **36**

Theme Park

See also Leisure Park

Flambards Village — 3D **7**
Spirit of the West American Theme Park — 1B **12**

Vineyard

See also Cidermaker

Camel Valley Vineyard — 1C **13**
Clawford Vineyard — 3B **26**
Down St Mary Vineyard & Winery — 3B **28**
Highfield Vineyards — 2D **29**
Moorlynch Vineyard — 3D **37**
Polmassick Vineyard — 3B **12**
Porthallow Vineyard & Cider Farm — 2B **8**
Sharpham Vineyard — 2C **17**
Staplecombe Vineyards — 1C **31**
Veryan Vineyard — 3B **12**

Visitor Centre/Information Centre

Axminster Carpets Visitor Centre — 1C **25**
Barbican Glassworks — Plymouth
Berry Head Country Park Visitor Centre, Brixham
    — 2D **17**
Blackdown Hills Interpretation Centre, Clayhidon
    — 2B **30**
Boscastle Visitor Centre — 1D **19**
Bude Visitor Centre — Bude
Burrows Centre, Northam — 3C **33**
Cannington Countryside Visitor Centre — 3C **37**
Charmouth Heritage Coast Centre — 1D **25**
Clovelly Centre, The — 1B **26**

Cockington Country Park Visitor Centre — 1C **17**
Cornwall Industrial Discovery Centre, Pool — 1D **7**
Daphne du Maurier Literary Centre, The — Fowey
Dawlish Warren Local Nature Reserve Visitor Centre
    — 3D **23**
Delabole Wind Farm Renewable Energy Centre
    — 2C **19**
Eggesford Country Centre — 2A **28**
Fyne Court Visitor Centre — 3C **37**
Gwennap Pit Visitor Centre, St Day — 3D **11**
Hinkley Point Visitor Centre — 2C **37**
Isles of Scilly Wildlife Trust Visitor Centre,
    Hugh Town, St. Mary's, Isles of Scilly — 1B **66**
Lizard Countryside Centre, The, Garras — 2B **8**
Maunsel Canal Centre — 1D **31**
Mayflower Visitor Centre — Plymouth
Meldon Viaduct & Quarry Visitors Centre — 1D **21**
Mineral Tramways Discovery Centre, The, Brea
    — 1D **7**
Mount Edgcumbe Country Park Information Centre,
    Cremyll — 2C **15**
North Cornwall Wildlife Information Centre,
    Wadebridge — 3B **18**
Okehampton Station Visitor Centre — 1D **21**
Peat Moors Visitor Centre — 2D **37**
Polzeath Visitor Centre — 3B **18**
Porlock Visitor Centre — 2C **35**
Quantock Information Centre — 3B **36**
Quay House Visitor Centre — Exeter
St Austell Brewery Visitor Centre — 2C **13**
Siblyback Lake Visitor Centre, St Cleer — 3A **20**
Slapton Ley Field Centre — 2C **17**
Somerset Levels & Moors Visitor Centre — 2D **37**
South East Cornwall Discovery Centre — Looe
Stover Country Park Ranger's Office, Heathfield
    — 3C **23**
Tamar Lakes Water Park Interpretation Centre,
    Alfardisworthy — 2A **26**
Tarka Trail (Railway Carriage) Visitor Centre,
    Bideford — 1C **27**
Town & Countryside Centre, Bodmin — Bodmin
Wembury Marine Centre — 3D **15**
West Somerset Railway Visitor Centre,
    Bishops Lydeard — 1B **30**
Wimbleball Water Park Information Kiosk,
    Brompton Regis — 3D **35**

Wildlife Park

See also Animal Collection, Farm Park, Zoo

Alstone Wildlife Park — 2D **37**
Combe Martin Wildlife & Dinosaur Park — 2A **34**
Cricket St Thomas Wildlife Park — 3D **31**
Dartmoor Wildlife Park — 2D **15**
Porfell Animal Land Wildlife Park — 2D **13**
Tropiquaria — 2A **36**

Windmill

See also Industrial Monument

Ashton (Chapel Allerton) Towermill — 1D **37**
Stembridge (High Ham) Towermill NT — 3D **37**

Zoo/Safari Park

See also Animal Collection, Farm Park, Wildlife Park

Exmoor Zoological Park — 2A **34**
Newquay Zoo — Newquay
Paignton Zoo Environmental Park — 2C **17**

Photo credits:

Barnabys Picture Library — Front Cover (Top) St. Ives (bottom) River Fowey; P.1 St Michaels Mount; P.4 North Cornish Coast; P.39 (bottom right) Clovelly; P.41 Brixham; P.44 Exeter Cathedral, Tudor Buildings Exeter; P.45 Dart Valley; P.47 River Fowey; P.55 Padstow Harbour; P.58 Plymouth Barbican, Drake Island Plymouth; P.59 Smeaton's Tower, The Hoe Plymouth; P.60 St. Ives.

Corbis Images — P.39 (bottom left) Hartland Point, Bryan Pickering; P.40 Cornish Countryside, Andrew Brown; P.42 Coastline Cornwall, Sally A. Morgan; P.43 River Dart, Patrick Ward; P.49 Ilfracombe, Paul Thompson; P.54 Fore Street, Totnes, Ric Ergenbright; P. 63 Torbay Harbour, Bryan Pickering; P.64 Bodmin Moor, Andrew Brown; P.65 Portchapel Beach, Adam Woolfit.